COUNTRIES OF THE WORLD

Kazakhstan

Gareth Stevens Publishing
A WORLD ALMANAC EDUCATION GROUP COMPANY

About the Author: Lily Loy was born and raised in Singapore. A professional language teacher, she has studied and worked in France and Latvia. In 1994, Loy spent two months in Kazakhstan doing volunteer work. She has also visited Russia and other former Soviet republics. Lily Loy currently lives in Singapore, where she teaches French.

PICTURE CREDITS

AFP: 37, 77, 78, 79, 84
ANA Picture Agency: 38
Art Directors & Trip Photo Library: cover, 1, 2, 3 (top), 4, 6, 11, 18, 21 (bottom), 23, 24, 25, 26 (bottom), 27, 28, 31, 32, 33, 39, 40, 42, 44, 48, 49, 52, 54, 55, 56, 57, 68, 71, 72, 73
Camera Press: 15 (center)
James Davis Worldwide: 13
Diplomatic Mission of the Republic of Kazakhstan to the Republic of Singapore: 10, 15 (top), 17, 34, 36, 45, 59, 60, 61, 62, 63, 64, 65, 76, 80, 81, 85
Eurasian Media: 15 (bottom)
Getty Images: 12, 75
HBL Network Photo Agency: 3 (bottom), 7, 26 (top), 30, 35, 46, 53, 67, 89
Hutchison Picture Library: 5, 8, 16, 20, 21 (top), 22, 47, 69, 70, 91
Marshall Cavendish International (Asia): 90 (both)
Buddy Mays: 29
Peggy McNamara: 43
Yumi Ng: 41
Simon Richmond: 58, 66, 74
Gerry Roach: 50
Steve Tonry: 14, 51
Still Pictures: 3 (center), 9, 19, 82
U.S. Peace Corps: 83

Digital Scanning by Superskill Graphics Pte Ltd

Written by
LILY LOY

Edited by
YUMI NG

Edited in the U.S. by
**CATHERINE GARDNER
ALAN WACHTEL**

Designed by
LYNN CHIN

Picture research by
**THOMAS KHOO
JOSHUA ANG**

First published in North America in 2005 by
Gareth Stevens Publishing
A World Almanac Education Group Company
330 West Olive Street, Suite 100
Milwaukee, Wisconsin 53212 USA

Please visit our web site at
www.garethstevens.com
For a free color catalog describing
Gareth Stevens Publishing's list of high-quality
books and multimedia programs, call
1-800-542-2595 (USA) or 1-800-387-3178 (Canada)
Gareth Stevens Publishing's fax: (414) 332-3567.

© **MARSHALL CAVENDISH INTERNATIONAL (ASIA) PRIVATE LIMITED 2004**
Originated and designed by
Times Editions Marshall Cavendish
An imprint of Marshall Cavendish International (Asia) Pte Ltd
A member of Times Publishing Limited
Times Centre, 1 New Industrial Road
Singapore 536196
http://www.timesone.com.sg/te

Library of Congress Cataloging-in-Publication Data
Loy, Lily.
Kazakhstan / by Lily Loy.
p. cm. -- (Countries of the world)
Includes bibliographical references and index.
ISBN 0-8368-3116-0 (lib. bdg.)
1. Kazakhstan--Juvenile literature.
I. Title. II. Countries of the world (Milwaukee, Wis.)
DK903.L69   2004
958.45--dc22   2004045319

Printed in Singapore

1 2 3 4 5 6 7 8 9 08 07 06 05 04

Contents

AN OVERVIEW OF KAZAKHSTAN

Kazakhstan, the largest of the Central Asian republics, was part of the Union of Soviet Socialist Republics (USSR) until 1991. For centuries, the Kazakhs, a nomadic people of Mongol and Turkic origin, herded livestock across the vast steppes of Kazakhstan in search of grazing land. At one time a part of Genghis Khan's legendary Mongol Empire, Kazakhstan came under Russian control in the eighteenth century. The arrival of hundreds of thousands of Slavic immigrants into Kazakhstan in the nineteenth and twentieth centuries changed the country's cultural and social scene. Kazakhstan's main challenge today is to maintain harmony among its multiethnic citizens, while using the country's natural resources for the benefit of all Kazakhstanis.

Opposite: Two Kazakh women walk by one of the restored towers of the Khoja Akhmed Yasavi Mausoleum in Turkestan.

Below: Ethnic Kazakh youngsters accompanied by their grandmother watch a parade. In Kazakhstan, elderly people are greatly respected, and grandparents often play an active role in raising children.

THE FLAG OF KAZAKHSTAN

The flag of Kazakhstan has a light blue background that represents the sky. In the center of the flag, a golden sun with thirty-two rays sits above a golden steppe eagle. The eagle's wings are outstretched, suggesting the image of an eagle soaring above Kazakhstan's vast steppes. A vertical band of golden Kazakh national ornamentation runs along the hoist side of the flag. The flag of Kazakhstan was adopted in June 1992. Before becoming independent, Kazakhstan, along with all former Soviet states, used the Soviet flag, which consisted of a red background with a yellow hammer, sickle, and star on the hoist side.

Geography

The Republic of Kazakhstan is the largest nation in Central Asia and the ninth-largest country in the world, with a total area of 1,030,810 square miles (2,669,800 square kilometers). Kazakhstan's neighbors are Russia, to the north and northwest; China, to the east; and Turkmenistan, Kyrgyzstan, and Uzbekistan to the south. The Caspian Sea and the Aral Sea, two of the largest lakes in the world, respectively, form part of the country's western and southern borders.

Mountains and Steppes

Most of Kazakhstan's vast territory consists of flat plains, called steppes, and rolling hills. Kazakhstan's spectacular mountain ranges account for only one-fifth of the country's total land area.

The Altai Mountains, an isolated mountain range that covers the junction where China, Kazakhstan, Mongolia, and Russia meet, dominate Kazakhstan's northeast. In the southeast, the Dzungarian Alatau forms a natural border with China. The Tien

Opposite: **Because of Kazakhstan's low rainfall and vast plains, its rivers often dry up before reaching any large body of water.**

THE DESERTS OF KAZAKHSTAN

Vast regions of desert land cover Kazakhstan's central and southern regions. Vegetation grows very sparsely in these deserts.
(A Closer Look, page 52)

Below: **A horseman travels Kazakhstan's vast steppes near the Altai Mountains.**

Shan, a mountain range that spans the borders between China, Kazakhstan, and Kyrgyzstan, is home to Mount Khan-Tengri, Kazakhstan's highest point, at 22,949 feet (6,995 meters).

The dominant feature of the Balkash Basin, a vast steppe in southeastern Kazakhstan, are its many lakes and rivers, which flow into Lake Balkash. Further inland, arid deserts, such as the Betpak Dala, extend over central Kazakhstan. The immense Saryarka Plains, which unfold to the north of the Betpak Dala, form one-fifth of the country's total land area. The foothills of the southern Urals, known as the Mugodzhari Hills, form a natural border between the deserts of central Kazakhstan and the Caspian Depression, a lowland surrounding the Caspian Sea.

Rivers and Lakes

Low annual rainfall keeps Kazakhstan's rivers from becoming major sources of water. The Seven Rivers region in the east is Kazakhstan's largest river system. The main rivers in the north of the country are the Irtysh, the Ishim, and the Tobyl, which flow into the Arctic Sea. The Syr Darya and the Chu are the largest rivers in the otherwise dry southern region.

SEVEN RIVERS

The Seven Rivers region was named after the many lakes and seven major rivers in the area of Lake Balkash. The region is known as *Zhetysu* (JAY-tee-soo) in Kazakh and *Semirechie* (SEH-mee-REH-chee-eh) in Russian; both names mean "seven rivers." The seven rivers are the Aksu, Baskan, Bi, Ili, Karatal, Lepsi, and Sarakand.

THE ARAL SEA

Once the fourth-largest lake in the world, environmental pollution and poor irrigation practices have reduced the size of the Aral Sea drastically over the past three decades.
(A Closer Look, page 48)

Climate

Kazakhstan has hot summers and extremely cold winters. The average winter temperature in the north is 0° Fahrenheit (-18° Celsius), while in the south it is -26° F (-3°C). Temperatures in the north may drop to -49°F (-45°C) when icy winds blow in from Siberia. Summers in the south are hot and dry, and temperatures may rise to 84°F (29°C). The northern regions enjoy cooler summers, with temperatures rarely rising above 68°F (20°C). Kazakhstan suffers from a lack of rainfall. The steppe regions in the northern and central parts of the country receive about 8 to 12 inches (200 to 300 millimeters) of rain per year. Desert regions, especially around the Kyzylkum Desert and the Ustyurt Plateau in the southwest, are extremely dry.

Plants and Animals

Because of the country's varied landscapes and climates, Kazakhstan is home to a rich variety of plants and animals. Different varieties of grass, such as feather grass and oat grass, grow throughout the steppes and provide grazing land for

Opposite: **A snow leopard walks on the snowy surface of the Tien Shan.**

ENVIRONMENTAL PROBLEMS

Misuse of water and land resources in Kazakhstan during the Soviet era has caused serious environmental problems in the country. Nuclear weapons testing was also performed in Kazakhstan, causing serious damage to the environment and the people.
(A Closer Look, page 54)

Below: **Pine trees grow on snow-covered mountains near a ski resort in Astana.**

livestock. Different species of wormwood grow in deserts located near the steppes. Tough varieties of grass and shrubs survive in the country's clay and gravel deserts. The valleys in the Tien Shan region are lined with apple and other fruit trees. Birch and aspen groves grow in the cooler regions of the north, while pine forests are common in the valleys of the Irtysh and Tobyl Rivers.

Kazakhstan is home to countless species of animals. The rare saiga antelope, currently protected by law, roams the steppes of Kazakhstan along with other antelope and elk. Tortoises, snakes, and the world's largest lizard, the grey monitor lizard, often appear in the desert plains. The goitered gazelle can be spotted in the deserts and mountains near Lake Balkash. The Karakul sheep, originally from Tajikistan, grazes high up in the Altai and Tien Shan. The forests in the Tien Shan are also home to the lynx, the snow leopard, and the brown bear. Lake Tengiz provides a shelter for wild geese and ducks, as well as flamingos and herons. Larks and eagles are common in the open steppes. Seals and sturgeon abound in the Caspian Sea. Kazakhstan's rivers were once teeming with fish, but over the past decades, the fish population has decreased sharply due to water pollution.

MOUNTAIN VEGETATION

The main forests of Kazakhstan are found in the Altai Mountains, Dzungarian Alatau, and Zailiysky Alatau, the range of the Tien Shan found in Kazakhstan. Vegetation similar to the grasses found in the open steppes covers the foothills. Above the foothills, briar and honeysuckle mix with aspen and birch. In the forests of the Zailiysky Alatau, wild apple trees, apricot trees, and other fruit trees grow. Further up, coniferous forests are a common sight. The Altai range supports a rich variety of trees, such as the Siberian larch, spruce, fir, and cedar.

History

Early History

By about 2000 B.C., people of the Andronovo culture lived in present-day Kazakhstan. While most of these groups were nomadic and lived by raising cattle, some of them were sedentary and lived by farming the land. These peoples also knew how to mine metals and make weapons and utensils from bronze. In about 500 B.C., the Scythians, a nomadic people from Persia that excelled at horseback warfare, moved into Central Asia.

The Scythians were overthrown by the Usun, a Turkic-speaking people of Mongol ancestry. Over the next eight hundred years, other Turkic groups gained control of the area. The Silk Road, the main trade route that connected China to Europe, cut through the southern region of present-day Kazakhstan. Arabs traveling on this road had introduced Islam and Arab culture to Central Asia in the 700s. By the 1200s, Islam had become the religion of the people of Central Asia.

The Kazakh Empire

In the twelfth century, a mix of nomadic and sedentary tribes, headed by tribal leaders, occupied the territory of what is now Kazakhstan. From the twelfth to the fourteenth century, most of Central Asia was part of one of several Mongol khanates headed by the descendants of Genghis Khan. Tribal and clan leaders, however, continued to exert great power.

In the mid-1400s, a clan headed by Kirai and Janibek broke away from the Uzbek khan and settled in the southern part of the region. Because the people of this tribe were nomads, they were called Kazakh Uzbeks, meaning "nomadic Uzbeks," to tell them apart from the Uzbeks, who led sedentary lives. Scholars believe that the word *kazakh* (kah-ZAHK) means "free and independent nomad." Later, the Kazakh Uzbeks came to be called "Kazakhs."

During the fifteenth and sixteenth centuries, the Kazakhs developed a nomadic empire that extended throughout the steppes of present-day Kazakhstan. Under Kasim Khan, who ruled from 1509 to 1518, the empire grew and was feared by its neighbors. After Kasim Khan's death, the empire was divided into three subgroups, which became known as the Three Hordes.

Above: **A statue of Kenesary Kasimov (1802–1847), a great Kazakh leader, stands in a square in Almaty.**

THE THREE HORDES

When the Kazakh khanate split into three groups, each group was called *zhus* (ZHOOZ), which literally means "hundred." The Russian translation for zhus is *orda* (ohr-DAH), meaning "horde." The three groups were the Elder Horde of southern Kazakhstan and the Seven Rivers region, the Middle Horde of central and eastern Kazakhstan, and the Younger Horde of western Kazakhstan. Each of these hordes was further divided into ethnic groups, family clans, and family units.

Opposite: **The Khoja Akhmed Yasavi Mausoleum was built in the fourteenth century.**

THE GREAT DISASTER

In a series of battles between the 1680s and the 1720s, the Dzungars crushed the Kazakhs. The defeats cost the Kazakhs thousands of lives. The victory by the Dzungars is known in Kazakh history as the Great Disaster.

Mongol Attacks

From the late 1600s to the early 1700s, the Three Hordes were attacked by different Mongol tribes. Although the Three Hordes united to fight the Dzungars, a fierce Mongol tribe from the southeast, the hordes were devastated. Unable to defeat the Dzungars, the Kazakh khans sought the help of their powerful neighbors in the Russian and Chinese empires.

Russian Rule

The Russians regarded the Dzungars' expansion into what is now Kazakhstan as a threat to their security, so they began building forts in the north of the region in order to protect Russia's southern borders. Between 1731 and 1742, the khans of the Three Hordes pledged their allegiance to Russia in exchange for protection against the Dzungars.

The Russian empire abolished the Three Hordes and took over control of their territory. Many Kazakhs rebelled against Russian rule, but these rebellions were quickly put down. The Kazakh tribal leaders began to send their children to Russian schools, and soon a Kazakh intellectual elite was formed. Many of these intellectuals became Kazakh nationalists.

KENESARY KASIMOV

In the late 1830s, Kenesary Kasimov, a grandson of Ablai, a prominent leader of the Middle Horde, led a revolt against the Russians. Kasimov demanded that rule of Kazakhstan be returned to the Kazakhs. In 1844, Russian troops put down Kasimov's rebellion. Nevertheless, many Kazakhs supported Kasimov and were inspired by his bravery. Kazakh poets wrote poems that praised Kasimov's strength and courage.

In 1891, Russia passed a law that allocated a fixed area of land to each Kazakh household. All remaining land was redistributed by the government to Russian and Slavic farmers. This law forced the Kazakhs to abandon their nomadic lifestyle and live a sedentary life. Those Kazakhs who received poor farming and grazing land suffered. During World War I, Russia tried to enlist Kazakh men to fight against the Germans. The Kazakhs rebelled, but their revolt was crushed in 1916. Thousands of Kazakhs fled to China.

Soviet Rule

The Russian Revolution of 1917 ended czarist rule in Russia. After the communist Bolsheviks took control of Russia, Kazakh nationalists demanded independence. In 1917, the Kazakhs installed a nationalist government in Almaty headed by the Alash Orda party. This government was short-lived, and in 1920, the land of the Kazakhs became an autonomous republic under Soviet control. In 1936, the country became a republic of the Union of Soviet Socialist Republics, under which the Communist Party became the only political party allowed.

THE ALASH ORDA

The Alash Orda party was founded in 1905. After the Russian Revolution of 1917, the Alash governed Kazakhstan for a brief period before it became a republic under Soviet control. In the 1930s, Soviet leader Joseph Stalin ordered the arrest of most of the Alash Orda intellectuals. Many of them died in prison.

COLLECTIVIZATION

In 1929, Joseph Stalin introduced a drastic program of economic restructuring in the Soviet Union. Through this program, known as "collectivization," the government took over all farms and agricultural lands from the owners and relocated all farmers and their families onto large government farms. When Kazakh nomads refused to abandon their lifestyle, the Soviets reacted violently. Between 1926 and 1939, more than 1.5 million Kazakhs died of starvation or disease, or while in prison, as a result of harsh Soviet policies.

Left: This statue of Vladimir Lenin, leader of the Russian Revolution, stood opposite a government building in Atyrau. The statue was taken down after the collapse of the Soviet Union in the early 1990s.

Kazakhstan's Importance to the USSR

Under the Soviets, Kazakhstan's lands were opened up for agriculture. Kazakhstan also became a supplier of metals and fuel for the Soviet Union. Exploitation of Kazakhstan's resources resulted in great environmental damage. Semey, formerly known as Semipalatinsk, was used as a testing ground for nuclear weapons, which caused great radiation damage in the area.

Independence

Kazakhstan proclaimed independence on December 16, 1991, shortly before the dissolution of the Soviet Union. Kazakhstan, along with Russia and ten other former Soviet republics, formed the Commonwealth of Independent States (CIS) after the collapse of the USSR. Nursultan Abishevich Nazarbayev, the first secretary of the Communist Party of Kazakhstan, became Kazakhstan's first president. In the years following Kazakhstan's independence, the country experienced great social and economic upheaval, mostly due to the withdrawal of Soviet financial support. Over the past few years, however, Kazakhstan's situation has improved, thanks to foreign investment and political stability. Astana replaced Almaty as the capital of Kazakhstan in December 1997.

Above: The war memorial in Almaty stands opposite the Orthodox Svyato-Voznesensky Cathedral.

VIRGIN AND IDLE LANDS PROGRAM

In 1953, the government introduced a plan to increase the production of crops in the USSR. This plan, known as the Virgin and Idle Lands Program, designated the plains of Kazakhstan for agriculture. Thousands of immigrants poured into Kazakhstan to work on the lands.

ALMATY

The former capital of Kazakhstan, the city of Almaty has a long history. Almaty continues to be Kazakhstan's biggest city.

(*A Closer Look,* page 44)

Alikhan Bukeikhanov (1869–1932)

The founder of the Alash Orda Party, Bukeikhanov was a staunch Kazakh nationalist. A contributor to the nationalist magazine *Qazak*, he believed that in order to protect Kazakh culture and lifestyle from Russian suppression, all Kazakhs needed to unite and work together. In 1905, the czarist government allowed the creation of an assembly called the Duma, which consisted of elected representatives from the Russian Empire. Bukeikhanov, as a member of the Constitutional Democrat party, took part in sessions of the Duma but was arrested twice because of his opposition to the czar. After the Russian Revolution, Bukeikhanov agreed to serve in the Bolshevik government as a Kazakh representative.

Alikhan Bukeikhanov

Dinmukhamed Kunayev (1912–1993)

Born in Almaty, Kunayev worked in the mining industry before joining the Communist Party of the Soviet Union in 1939. In 1955, Kunayev was promoted to chairman of the Council of Ministers. Kunayev played a crucial role in implementing the Virgin and Idle Lands program, after being chosen as first secretary of the Communist Party of Kazakhstan in late 1959. Kunayev served as first secretary from 1960 to 1962 and 1964 to 1986. In order to maintain ethnic harmony in Kazakhstan, Kunayev, a native Kazakh, was careful to grant equal treatment to both Kazakhs and Russians. In 1986, Soviet leader Mikhail Gorbachev removed Kunayev from office amid violent protests from the people of Kazakhstan.

Dinmukhamed Kunayev

Dariga Nazarbayeva (1963–)

The eldest of President Nursultan Nazarbayev's three daughters, Nazarbayeva has begun to play an increasingly important role in Kazakhstan's public life. Some observers believe that Nazarbayev is grooming his daughter to be his successor. In 2003, Nazarbayeva founded Asar, a new political party that means "all together." Originally founded as an organization committed to helping the poor, Asar became a political party a few months later. Nazarbayeva is also chairwoman of the Executive Committee of the Congress of Kazakhstan Journalists.

Dariga Nazarbayeva

Government and the Economy

Kazakhstan is a parliamentary republic headed by a president. The government consists of three branches: the executive branch, the legislative branch, and the judicial branch. Kazakhstan is divided into fourteen *oblystar* (oh-blees-TAHR), or provinces. Three cities, Astana, Almaty, and Baikonyr, hold the same status as the oblystar. All Kazakhstanis age eighteen years old and older have the right to vote in elections.

The executive branch consists of the president and a council of ministers, which is headed by a prime minister. The legislative branch is made up of two houses, an upper house called the Senate and a lower house called the *Majilis* (mah-jee-LEES). The Senate has thirty-nine members, seven of whom are directly appointed by the president. The remaining senate members are elected by the people to serve six-year terms. The assembly consists of seventy-seven members, ten of whom belong to the ruling party. Assembly members are elected by popular vote to

POLITICAL PARTIES

Kazakhstan's main political parties are the Agrarian Party; the Ak Zhol, or "White Road," Party; the AUL "Village" Party; the Civic Party; the Communist Party, or KPK; the Otan "Fatherland"; and the Patriots' Party. Some opposition party leaders have claimed that a law passed in 2002 aims to wipe out opposition parties in Kazakhstan, as this law sets out criteria for political parties, such as having 50,000 members, that few parties are able to meet.

serve five-year terms. The judicial branch consists of the Supreme Court, which has forty-four members, and the Constitutional Council, which has seven members. The Constitutional Council, a part of the judicial branch, was created in 1995. The president appoints the chairman of the council, while the president, the chairman of the Senate, and the chairman of the Majilis each nominate two members. Council members serve six-year terms. One of the council's duties is to settle disputes concerning elections. The council also makes sure that all laws passed by parliament and all international treaties signed by the president are in accordance with Kazakhstan's constitution.

The President of Kazakhstan

In 1995, President Nazarbayev expanded the powers of the president of Kazakhstan by introducing amendments to the country's constitution. According to Kazakhstan's new constitution, the president may dissolve parliament, start constitutional reforms, call for a referendum, and appoint provincial and city leaders. The president also appoints the prime minister and the council of ministers.

Above: **Police officers help to control traffic in Kazakhstan.**

NURSULTAN NAZARBAYEV

The leader of Kazakhstan since 1990, Nazarbayev further strengthened his powers through amendments to the country's constitution in 1995. One of the president's main challenges is to find responsible ways of using the country's vast mineral riches.
(*A Closer Look, page 64*)

Opposite: **This modern building in Astana houses the offices of the president of Kazakhstan and the council of ministers.**

Economy

Kazakhstan is rich in natural resources, with vast oil reserves and agricultural regions. During the Soviet years, Kazakhstan supplied raw materials to the Soviet Union in exchange for manufactured goods. After Kazakhstan became independent, the country's economy declined, as Soviet demand for its products fell sharply. Since the mid-1990s, due to foreign investment, economic restructuring, growth in the energy sector, and good harvests, Kazakhstan's economy has improved. In 2002, the economy grew by 9.5 percent.

Above: **A worker checks the condition of a metal train wheel in a railway workshop located in the Akmola province. Kazakhstan is a major producer of metals.**

Natural Resources

Energy resources are Kazakhstan's most important economic assets. The country has enormous reserves of coal, natural gas, and oil. The most important oil and gas resources are found in Tengiz, in western Kazakhstan. Kazakhstan is also rich in minerals and metals such as chromium, copper, gold, iron, nickel, and uranium.

TRADITIONAL ECONOMY

Kazakhs in some rural areas continue to raise livestock for a living, using some of the same methods favored by their ancestors.
(A Closer Look, page 68)

Agriculture

In 2002, agriculture accounted for 9 percent of Kazakhstan's gross domestic product (GDP). Kazakhstan is the world's sixth-largest producer of grain, including wheat and barley. Kazakhstan's main farming regions are located in the north-central and southern parts of the country. The north-central region focuses on grain production, while the southern region produces mostly cotton and rice, two other major crops. A large part of Kazakhstan's agricultural lands are used as pastureland for livestock.

Industry

Machine building and metal working plants were the main industries in Kazakhstan during Soviet times. At present, the government is expanding the manufacture of household and consumer goods, with the help of foreign investors.

Transportation

Railway tracks run between Kazakhstan's major cities. Over the past few years, foreign firms have financed the development of many of the country's new networks of roads. Air Astana flies to other CIS states, as well as to other Asian countries and Europe.

OIL PIPELINES

Because Kazakhstan is landlocked, the country needs to build pipelines (*below*) to transport its oil resources to other countries. Major oil firms from the United States and other countries have invested in the building of pipelines in Kazakhstan since the 1990s. A 980-mile (1,580-km) pipeline that links the Tengiz oil field in Kazakhstan's Caspian Sea region to the Russian port of Novorossiysk on the Black Sea began operations in 2001. China and Kazakhstan have also begun building a 1,860-mile (3,000-km) pipeline from Atyrau, a city along the Caspian Sea, to the Xinjiang province, in western China.

People and Lifestyle

A multiethnic society, Kazakhstan has a population of about 16.8 million. The indigenous Kazakhs are a mixture of the Turkic and Mongol peoples who have populated Central Asia for centuries. Ethnic Kazakhs make up just over half of the country's total population, while the remaining half consists of Kazakhstanis of Russian, Ukrainian, Uzbek, German, Korean, and other ancestry.

Changing Demographics

Although the Kazakhs were the original inhabitants of Kazakhstan, by the latter half of the twentieth century, they had become a minority. From the Russians' arrival in Kazakhstan in the 1800s to the time of the Virgin and Idle Lands Program in the 1950s, thousands of Russian and other immigrants came to work in industry and agriculture in Kazakhstan. Germans and Koreans living in Soviet-occupied regions were sent to Kazakhstan by the government. On the other hand, during the first half of the twentieth century, thousands of Kazakhs either died of starvation during the land reform programs or were killed during Stalin's purges. Many Kazakhs who survived emigrated to China.

Since independence, the demographic balance in Kazakhstan has begun to change again. Thousands of ethnic Kazakhs have returned from China and other Central Asian nations. At the same time, since the fall of the Soviet Union, as many as one million Russians, Germans, and Ukrainians have left Kazakhstan.

Although Kazakhs now form the majority in Kazakhstan as a whole, Russians continue to be the majority group in the country's large cities.

Social Challenges in Kazakhstan

The change in demographics in Kazakhstan has created a number of social and economic problems. The emigration of Russians, Germans, and Ukrainians out of Kazakhstan has left the country with a shortage of skilled labor, as many of the emigrants worked in industry. The ethnic Kazakhs who have returned find it difficult to adjust to life in Kazakhstan as they do not speak Russian, the language of business in Kazakhstan.

Above: **A Slavic Kazakhstani man (*top*) wears a fur hat to keep warm in winter, while a Tatar Kazakhstani woman (*bottom*) enjoys a day out in Almaty.**

MULTIETHNIC NATION

The arrival of Russians in Kazakhstan turned the country into a nation of various ethnic groups, including Russians and Germans in addition to ethnic Kazakhs.
(A Closer Look, page 58)

Opposite: **An ethnic Kazakh family poses for a photograph in a public square.**

Family Life

Family ties are extremely important to Kazakhs. Traditionally, every Kazakh was expected to know the names of at least seven generations of ancestors on the father's side. This tradition continues in some Kazakh families today. All ethnic Kazakhs claim descent from one of the Three Hordes. Each Horde was divided into tribes. These tribes were not necessarily blood-related, and each tribe was made up of a number of family clans.

Traditional Kazakh Marriages

In the past, most Kazakh marriages were arranged. The groom's family paid a bride price, or *kalym* (kah-LEEM), to the bride's family, while the bride was expected to bring a dowry to the marriage. Another Kazakh tradition was "bride kidnapping," or *alyp qashu* (ah-LIP kah-SHOE). Many of these kidnappings, however, were done with the consent of the bride, usually in cases when the bride's parents opposed the marriage. According to Kazakh tradition, a rich man could have more than one wife. Payment of a bride price, bride kidnapping, and polygamy

Left: **A Kazakh man takes his baby for a walk in one of Almaty's public squares.**

Left: Kazakh children share family responsibilities, such as taking care of younger siblings.

YURTAS

A *yurta* (yoor-TAH), or circular tent, is the traditional Kazakh nomadic dwelling. Made from animal skins or felt stretched over a frame of poles, Kazakh nomads assembled and disassembled these tents as they moved from place to place.
(*A Closer Look, page 72*)

became illegal in the early 1920s, after the Soviets came to power. These marriage traditions, however, still occur in Kazakhstan's remote rural areas.

In traditional Kazakh society, the eldest son usually marries first. He leaves his parental home to set up his own household, while the youngest son usually inherits the family home. The youngest son is expected to take care of his elderly parents.

Kazakh Children

Couples with three to four children are common in rural areas; in cities, most couples have only one or two children. The birth rate is higher among Kazakhs than among other ethnic groups.

In the countryside, Kazakh children are trained to work from a very young age. Boys learn to ride on horseback and look after livestock. In fact, Kazakhs sometimes say that Kazakh boys learn how to ride before they learn how to walk. In the past, girls were married off as soon as they reached adolescence. These days, girls in the countryside usually do not marry until they are at least in their late teens, while girls in the cities usually marry when they are at least in their twenties.

WOMEN IN KAZAKHSTAN

Since independence, women in Kazakhstan have faced many challenges. During the economic crisis of the early 1990s, many women were not able to find jobs. The situation was especially critical for elderly women and single mothers.
(*A Closer Look, page 70*)

Education

Education is compulsory and free of charge, from preschool to high school, for all children in Kazakhstan. Over the past few years, the government has introduced a new education system to replace the Soviet system. Under the new system, schools consist of twelve grades and are divided into primary (first to fourth grades), basic (fifth to ninth grades), and high (tenth to twelfth grades) segments. Children start school at the age of six or seven. Children enrolled in the first and second grades in 2004 are already under the new system.

Most students in Kazakhstan in 2004, however, still follow the old system, which consists of eleven grades. In general, the first five years are considered the primary years, while the last six years are considered the secondary years. During the Soviet era, illiteracy was almost completely wiped out. Kazakhstan's literacy rate is 98.4 percent for all adults age fifteen and older.

Higher Education

Kazakhstanis greatly value higher education. After graduating from school, students wishing to go to a university must take

Above: **Kazakhstani men and women majoring in accounting take a computer course in Karaganda. The literacy rate in Kazakhstan is close to one hundred percent.**

Opposite: **Al-Farabi Kazakh National University's campus in Almaty is surrounded by breathtaking natural scenery.**

exams on three different subjects. Two of these exams are on general subjects, such as math and history. The third exam is on a subject, such as chemistry, that is related to the student's choice of university major. In addition, non-Kazakh students must take a basic Kazakh language exam, while Kazakh students must take an advanced Kazakh language exam. The Al-Farabi Kazakh National University and the East Kazakhstan State University are among the most famous universities in Kazakhstan. Vocational schools, where students learn practical subjects such as electronics, are also popular.

Challenges in Education

After Kazakhstan became an independent nation, its education system went through a difficult period. Until 1990, all schools in Kazakhstan were entirely funded by the Soviet government. Independence meant that the schools could no longer depend on Soviet funds. Schools suffered from poor maintenance and lack of textbooks. The infrastructure of the schools in Kazakhstan has improved over the last few years, as new schools have been built and old schools have been refurbished.

MULTILINGUAL EDUCATION

During the Soviet period, all classes were taught in Russian. Since independence, some schools have begun teaching all subjects in Kazakh, although learning Russian is also compulsory. On the other hand, Russian schools in Kazakhstan are required to teach Kazakh language classes. Schools where classes are taught in the languages of Kazakhstan's minority groups, such as Uzbek, Uighur, Tajik, and Ukrainian, have also opened.

Religion

Kazakhstan is a secular state, and the constitution of Kazakhstan guarantees freedom of religion. Almost half of Kazakhstan's population is Muslim, while 44 percent is Russian Orthodox. The Muslim population includes Kazakhs and other Central Asian peoples. The remaining population consists of Roman Catholics, Protestants, Jews, and followers of other religions.

Muslim Kazakhs and Orthodox Christian Russians have lived peacefully side by side for more than two hundred years in Kazakhstan. During the Soviet period, the government discouraged religious practices, replacing them with social activities. Since independence, religion has been gaining importance in Kazakhstan. Nevertheless, society in Kazakhstan remains thoroughly secularized. Kazakhstan has no Islamic political party, and religious holidays are not national holidays.

Above: **Muslim Kazakh men gather at a mosque in Semey.**

Islam

Most Kazakhs are Sunni Muslim. Although the Kazakhs embraced Islam in the thirteenth century, until the nineteenth century, most Kazakhs had very little knowledge of the Qur'an, Islam's holy book, and Islamic religious practices. Because most Kazakhs led nomadic lives on the steppes, far away from cities

NATIVE KAZAKH BELIEFS

For hundreds of years, the nomadic Kazakhs practiced animism, shamanism, and ancestor worship. Even after the arrival of Islam, the Kazakhs continued to practice these beliefs. Kazakhs treasured their livestock and believed that spirits came to live in the animals. To this day, during special celebrations, a whole lamb is roasted and shared among family members and friends. Before partaking of the feast, a special prayer is said asking the spirit of the lamb for permission to eat its meat.

Left: **The majestic Central Mosque in Astana was built in 1999.**

and towns where mosques and religious schools were located, most Kazakhs were nominal Muslim, and many kept indigenous Kazakh traditions and beliefs.

In the nineteenth century, czarist Russia used Islam as a means of unifying and civilizing the Central Asian nomads. Tatar Islamic teachers from west-central Russia and religious leaders from the neighboring Central Asian nations provided Islamic instruction to the Kazakhs.

Other Religious Groups

Members of the Russian Orthodox Church in Kazakhstan consist mostly of ethnic Russians and other Slavic peoples, such as Ukrainians. Other Christian groups present in Kazakhstan are Roman Catholics, Lutherans, and Baptists. All religious groups in Kazakhstan are required to register with a government agency. The country's government has jailed religious workers whose congregations were not registered. Kazakhstan's Jewish community is decreasing in number as Kazakhstani Jews have been moving to Israel and the United States. Currently, between fifteen thousand and twenty thousand Jews live in Kazakhstan.

Above: **Kazakhstani Russians attend a Christmas service at a Russian Orthodox church in Akmola.**

ISLAMIC REVIVAL IN KAZAKHSTAN

Although Kazakhs are mostly a Muslim people, the government of Kazakhstan is concerned about the spread of Muslim extremism in the country. Islamic extremist groups, such as Hizb ut-Tahrir, or Islamic Party of Liberation, have been distributing leaflets and other extremist literature in Kazakhstan since 2000. In November 2003, the Kazakhstani police located a Hizb ut-Tahrir cell in the town of Pavlodar.

Language and Literature

Each ethnic group in Kazakhstan speaks a different language. The Kazakhs, the indigenous population of Kazakhstan, speak Kazakh. Over the two-hundred-year Russian domination of Kazakhstan, Russian became the language of instruction in schools and the common language among the country's different ethnic groups. Russian was the official language of Kazakhstan during the Soviet years.

After independence, Kazakh became an official language in the country. As most Russians and other groups do not know Kazakh, Russian also continues to be an official language and is used in business and for communication among Kazakhstanis. Other languages spoken in Kazakhstan include Uzbek, Tatar, and Uighur, which are similar to Kazakh. The Ukrainian and German minorities speak their own languages, as well as Russian.

The Kazakh Language

Kazakh, which is a Turkic language, contains many words from Russian and Arabic, as well as Mongol, Persian, and other Turkic

The first Kazakh writers emerged in the latter half of the nineteenth century. These writers were educated in Russian schools.

Considered the father of modern Kazakh literature, Abay Kunanbayev (1845–1904), the son of a tribal leader, was the creator of the modern style of Kazakh verse.

The best-known Kazakh literary figure of the Soviet period is Mukhtar Auezov (1897–1961). Auezov's best known work is *The Path of Abay*, a long epic poem based on Kunanbayev's life in the steppes in the late 1800s.

During the 1930s, Stalin jailed many Kazakh writers who promoted Kazakh culture, including Auezov.

Left: The Qur'an, Islam's holy book, is written in Arabic. In the 1860s, Kazakhs attempted to write in the Kazakh language using Arabic script.

languages. In recent years, English words related to information technology have been incorporated into the Kazakh language. In the 1860s, the Kazakh language was written down for the first time using Arabic script. In the 1920s, the Kazakhs briefly used the Latin alphabet. In 1940, the Cyrillic alphabet, used in Russian, was adopted, along with some extra symbols, to write Kazakh.

Literary Tradition

The Kazakhs have a rich oral heritage of epic tales and poems. Many of these tales tell the story of a heroic warrior, or *batyr* (bah-TEER), who defended the Kazakh tribes against Mongol invaders. Most of these epics and poems date back to the period between the fifteenth and sixteenth centuries. These works were handed down by word of mouth through the centuries by storytellers, who traveled from clan to clan reciting the tales, and poets, who often accompanied aristocratic clans traveling on the steppes. Famous epics include *Koblandy-Batir* and *Er Sain*, while *Kiz-Jhibek* is the most famous Kazakh love story. Kazakh poems were influenced by Sufi philosophy, a mystical form of Islam that sought to experience divine love through the senses.

HOW IS YOUR LIVESTOCK?

Because nomadic Kazakhs depended on livestock breeding for their livelihood, the Kazakh language has many expressions related to the raising of animals. "Are your livestock and your soul still healthy?" is a popular greeting among Kazakhs living in present-day rural Kazakhstan. "May God give you one thousand sheep with lambs, eighty camels, and eight married sons," is a traditional Kazakh wish of good fortune.

Arts

Kazakhstan has a rich artistic tradition that goes back to the beginning of civilization. Archaeologists have unearthed beautiful examples of carved metal ornaments in Kazakhstan that date back to 2000 B.C. For centuries, the nomadic Kazakhs created beautiful leather saddles for horseback riding and wove colorful rugs for their tents. The arrival of Russians into Kazakhstan in the nineteenth century brought into the country the elegance and skill of Russian ballet and music.

Above: **Two Kazakh girls show off their traditional attire during a festival.**

Opposite: **Traditional Kazakh carpets are colorful and display geometric designs. Kazakh homes are often decorated with handcrafted rugs.**

Kazakh Handicrafts

The Kazakhs excel at making folk handicrafts. As nomads, the Kazakhs lived far away from cities and towns, where household goods could be purchased. As a result, they learned to make items for everyday use, such as clothes, rugs, furniture, pots, saddles, and weapons, using materials within their reach.

In the past, carpet making involved a whole family's participation, from gathering hay and dyeing the wool, to cutting out pattern designs and sewing the patterns onto the rugs.

Woodworking was an important craft for the Kazakhs as wood was used to make the framework and panels of their tents. Kazakhs also crafted beautiful wooden furniture and chests.

Saddlemaking is an ancient craft among the Kazakhs, who are renowned horseback riders. To cope with the harsh climate of the steppes, the Kazakhs also used animal skins to make coats.

Silver is the most popular metal used in Kazakh jewelry. From ancient times, Kazakhs have also developed the crafts of making weapons, instruments, and household items from metal.

Architecture

Unlike other Central Asian nations, such as Uzbekistan, Kazakhstan does not have many ancient buildings or mosques. As nomads, the Kazakhs built very few permanent buildings. Nonetheless, southern Kazakhstan has fine examples of ancient structures, such as the Arystanbab Mosque, located near the city of Otrar Tobe, and the Khoja Akhmed Yasavi Mausoleum, in Turkestan. The Orthodox Svyato-Voznesensky Cathedral in Almaty is a fine example of Russian architecture in Kazakhstan.

ANCIENT AND MODERN ARCHITECTURE

Fine examples of ancient structures, such as old mud brick towns and mausoleums, are still found in Kazakhstan. Astana, the country's new capital, displays the latest architectural styles.
(A Closer Look, page 47)

TRADITIONAL CLOTHING

Traditional Kazakh clothes are colorful. Sewn from different types of fabrics, they are often decorated with intricate embroidery and felt patches.
(A Closer Look, page 66)

Traditional Music

Music plays a very important role in Kazakh society. In the past, a *zhyrau* (jeer-OW), or storyteller, would travel to different nomadic camps and sing verses from epic poems. An *akyn* (ah-KIN), or a poet-improviser, played the *dombra* (dome-BRAH), an instrument similar to the lute, to accompany improvised verses of poetry. These days, the zhyrau and the akyn perform at festivals and other special occasions. Folk songs are also popular. Women sing a cappella folk songs on special occasions, such as weddings, funerals, and religious holidays.

Modern Music

During Soviet times, the government encouraged professional training in music. A conservatory and several music colleges were set up, along with many art and music schools for children. The Zhambyl Philharmonic Society, which included a Kazakh choir, a folk music orchestra, and a folk dance ensemble, first formed in 1935. The society was housed in the Kazakh State Musical Theater, which was built in 1934 in Almaty. In 1945, the theater was renamed the Abay State Academic Opera and Ballet House of Kazakhstan, after writer Abay Kunanbayev.

MUSICAL INSTRUMENTS AND ORAL EPICS

Traditional Kazakh storytellers often accompanied their verses with music. The storytellers sang their epic poems while playing traditional Kazakh drums and stringed instruments. (*A Closer Look, page 60*)

Below: **A Kazakhstani children's ensemble performs traditional songs on dombras.**

Dance

Traditional Kazakh folk dancing is lively and full of bravura. Inspired by the nomadic lifestyle, Kazakh dances feature stylized portrayals of hunting and animal training, as well as other activities associated with the nomadic way of life, such as weaving. Kazakh dance has no formal rules. Dancers are allowed to improvise their acrobatic movements during a performance. Kazakhs enjoy watching an exciting dance in which the dancers stand on their saddles and dance on horseback. Unlike the dances of other Central Asian nations, many Kazakh dances feature boys and girls performing in pairs.

Although dance was never as important as music in traditional Kazakh society, professional theater formed in the 1930s. Those dances then became popular with folk groups. Like music, Kazakh dance adopted Russian themes and styles of expression. Operas and ballets were created based on traditional Kazakh themes. Today, classical ballet continues to flourish in Kazakhstan; Almaty is home to a professional ballet troupe.

Leisure and Festivals

Kazakhstanis living in the country's cities spend their leisure time in much the same way as people in other cities in the world. Most cities and towns in Kazakhstan have parks, and city dwellers often spend their weekends relaxing in the parks with friends and family. Urban Kazakhstanis are also fond of watching movies. Rural Kazakhs, on the other hand, enjoy gathering with friends and relatives, horseback riding, and attending lively festivals. Traditional Kazakh pastimes, such as poetry contests and games on horseback, while no longer practiced by the majority of Kazakhs, are still seen at festivals and fairs. Outdoor sports are popular with both urban and rural Kazakhstanis.

Berkutchi

For centuries, nomadic peoples of the Middle East and Central Asia have practiced hunting using various birds of prey. In Kazakhstan, the traditional sport of *berkutchi* (behr-koot-SHE) involves training a golden eagle to hunt. Riding on horseback, the trainer, who is called a berkutchi, goes to find a possible target.

Below: **A group of young Kazakhstanis enjoy sliding down a snowy slope at a ski resort near Astana.**

When the trainer spots a prey animal, he lets the eagle loose to fly after and catch the prey. Once the bird has caught the prey firmly in its claws without killing it, it flies back to its master and hands him the prey. Training a golden eagle to hunt is a very demanding and increasingly rare art.

Above: **A berkutchi must wear a thick leather glove in order to allow his golden eagle to perch on his right hand without cutting it.**

Poetry Contest

Aitys (eye-TEES) are formal or informal contests between two *akyndar* (ah-kin-DAHR) either of the same or opposite gender. Aitys test the poets' wit and skill in handling the Kazakh language. Nowadays held mostly as part of a festival or fair, aitys date back to ancient times. An akyn from each clan in a tribe took part in aitys, which were associated with shamanistic rituals. During an aitys, each poet cleverly makes up or improvises lyrics while playing the dombra. For instance, one singer may boast of his or her hometown or region, along with its sheep, horses, and people, and poke fun at his or her opponent's hometown. The opponent has to give a very quick, witty reply. The winner is the one who never hesitates to find quick, brilliant responses to his or her opponent's bantering, jesting, or unexpected questions.

KAZAKH GAMES

Most traditional Kazakh games developed from the nomadic Kazakh lifestyle. Many of these games involve displaying physical prowess on horseback.
(A Closer Look, page 57)

Sports

Kazakhstanis love sports and the outdoor life, and many of them are actively involved in sports. Favorite sports in the country include soccer, ice hockey, track, swimming, volleyball, basketball, Kazakh-style wrestling, weightlifting, and cycling. In recent years, skateboarding and in-line skating have become very popular among children and youths. The national sport of Kazakhstan is Kazakh-style wrestling, which is similar to judo.

Kazakhstan's snowy winters provide ideal conditions for the practice of winter sports. Ice skating and ice hockey are popular, since both can be practiced on many of the country's lakes and ponds, which freeze over in winter. The Medeo Sports Center, located near Almaty, amid breathtaking mountain scenery, boasts the largest mountain skating rink in the world. Skiing is also a popular sport, and the Chimbulak resort in the Tien Shan Mountains has become a popular ski resort area.

Professional Sports Training

During the Soviet years, Kazakhstan had numerous sports facilities, such as stadiums, public swimming pools, and

gymnasiums. After independence, some of these facilities had to close down because of a lack of government funds. Over the past few years, the government of Kazakhstan has tried to encourage Kazakhstan's youth to take up professional sports by funding sport schools, colleges, and boarding schools. Olympic training centers can be found in five provinces, with the Republic Olympic Training Center located in Almaty.

Above: **Kazakhstani sportswoman Olga Shishigina proudly displays her country's flag after winning the women's 100-meter hurdles race at the 2000 Olympic Games in Sydney, Australia.**

Outstanding Sports Figures

Since independence, Kazakhstani sports figures have excelled in many international competitions. Vladimir Smirnov won a gold medal for cross-country skiing at the 1994 Winter Olympic Games in Lillehammer, Norway. At the 2000 Summer Olympic Games in Sydney, Australia, Kazakh boxers won gold and silver medals in four different categories of boxing; Olga Shishigina won a gold medal in the women's 100-meter hurdles race; and Aleksandr Vinokurov won a silver medal in the men's road cycling race. Members of the Kazakhstan 2000 Olympics team took home a total of three gold and four silver medals.

ANATOLI BOUKREEV

A Russian by birth, Kazakhstani mountain climber Anatoli Boukreev reached the summits of the world's highest and toughest peaks.

(A Closer Look, page 50)

Secular Festivals

During the Soviet years, secular festivals replaced religious holidays in Kazakhstan because the Soviet regime discouraged the practice of religion. Although present-day Kazakhstan enjoys religious freedom, the government has been careful not to give any religious celebration the status of a public holiday, in order to maintain the separation between religion and state. Thus, Kazakhstan's public holidays, such as Independence Day, Republic Day, and Women's Day, are secular in nature.

Spring Festival

An ancient festival that probably originated in present-day Iran, Nauryz (now-REEZ) is the biggest festival in Kazakhstan. Nauryz is a public holiday that celebrates the beginning of spring and is held in the month of March.

On Nauryz, Kazakhstanis put on their best clothes and visit the homes of friends and relatives to exchange good wishes for the year ahead. Some Kazakhstanis don their finest traditional clothes. Stalls selling food and drink spring up on the streets, and traditional Kazakh games, such as singing competitions and

ISLAMIC CELEBRATIONS

Kazakhs observe the Islamic holiday of *Eid Al-Fitr* (EED ahl-feetr), as it is called in Arabic. Eid Al-Fitr, which is called *Oraza Ait* (OH-rah-zah AH-eet) in Kazakh, is the celebration that marks the end of Ramadan, the Islamic month of fasting. During Oraza Ait, Kazakhs prepare special foods, often slaughtering a sheep, and visit relatives and friends (*above*). Unlike in other Muslim countries, however, *Eid Al-Adha* (EED ahl-ahd-HAH), the festival of the sacrifice, is not a prominent holiday among Kazakh Muslims.

horseraces, take place in the city squares and stadiums. Families gather to partake of roasts and meat dishes, as well as cakes and sweets. The number seven has a special significance in Nauryz celebrations. For instance, the dishes served must be made from seven ingredients, and some people visit seven homes. Nauryz is also celebrated in some countries in the Middle East and Central Asia.

Zhas Kanat

Since its debut in 1992, the Zhas Kanat, or Voice of Asia, international music festival has become one of the most popular international events in Kazakhstan. Held at the Republic Palace in Almaty every year in the summer, aspiring young singers from Kazakhstan and other countries compete for trophies and cash prizes. The main goal of the event is to identify young talent. Many former participants have gone on to become famous singers in Kazakhstan and the other former Soviet states. Preliminary Zhas Kanat contests are held in cities throughout Kazakhstan; the winners then take part in the finals in Almaty. International stars perform as guests during the festival.

NAURYZ

A festival that marks the beginning of spring, Nauryz has been celebrated in Kazakhstan and other countries in Central Asia for hundreds of years.
(*A Closer Look*, page 62)

Below: **Kazakhstan's Russian community celebrates a festival in Astana.**

Food

Food is an important part of Kazakhstan's culture and heritage. As nomads, Kazakhs often spent months living isolated lives on the steppes with only their family or clan members to keep them company. Thus, receiving guests was a cause for great celebration. Although no longer nomads, present-day Kazakhs continue to practice their traditions of hospitality and often welcome their guests with sumptuous meals. In rural areas, Kazakhs still slaughter a lamb to be cooked and served in a guest's honor.

A Traditional Kazakh Meal

Meat, milk products, unleavened bread, and noodles are the traditional Kazakh staples. Meat is the most important part of a meal. Mutton is the most popular meat, and Kazakhs usually eat boiled mutton with dumplings or bread. Horseflesh is the most valued meat for the Kazakhs. Made from boiled mutton, beef, horseflesh, and noodles, *beshbarmak* (BESH-bahr-mahk) is Kazakhstan's national dish.

Below: **Pork sausages are popular among Kazakhstan's Slavic population. As Muslims, ethnic Kazakhs are not allowed to eat pork.**

Drinks

Kazakh traditional drinks are mostly milk- or yogurt-based. *Kymyz* (kur-MWEEZ) is a distinctive fermented Kazakh beverage made from mare's milk. *Boza* (boh-ZAH) is a millet-based alcoholic drink. Tea is the most common drink, and Kazakhs drink their tea with milk and sugar. Although not as popular as tea, coffee is also a common drink in Kazakhstan.

Above: Kazy (KAH-zee), smoked horseflesh sausage, is a Kazakh specialty. Kazy is often served thinly sliced.

Russian Influence and Other Cuisines

Present-day Kazakh cuisine consists of many dishes that have been adopted from Russian, Korean, and other Central Asian cuisines. Russian *borsch* (BOHRSH), a hearty soup made from meat boiled with beets, cabbage, potatoes, and sour cream, is very popular. *Pelmeni* (PEL-me-nee), a Russian dish that consists of meat and onion dumplings, is also common. Another popular dumpling is *manti* (mahn-TEE), a large dough pocket filled with meat, onions, and, occasionally, pumpkin. *Pilaf* (PEE-laf), or *plov* (PLOFF), is a rice dish made with carrots, mutton, and oil. The dish originally came from the Middle East. One popular version of pilaf is made with dried apples or apricots, raisins, and prunes.

A CLOSER LOOK AT KAZAKHSTAN

Kazakhstan is a country of many paradoxes. Within this vast nation, the present and the past coexist. While the country's modern cities of Almaty and Astana boast sleek examples of contemporary architecture, relics of majestic buildings, dating to the days when khans ruled the land, can still be visited in southern Kazakhstan. Although the majority of Kazakhs now lead sedentary lives, living and working in towns and villages, the country's nomadic heritage lives on in the many traditional games on horseback still played today, in the singing competitions, and in the ancient festivals, such as Nauryz.

Opposite: **A Slavic Kazakhstani woman runs a handicraft shop in the Akmola province. Kazakhstani women are well educated and contribute to the country's economy.**

From immense deserts and steppes to forests and picturesque lakes, Kazakhstan's landscape is also filled with contrasts. The country's towering snowcapped summits served as training grounds for Kazakhstani Anatoli Boukreev, one of the world's best-known mountaineers. Kazakhstan's varied and rich environment, however, has been badly damaged by poor irrigation practices, industrial pollution, and, most seriously, by nuclear testing. Nevertheless, Kazakhstan's rich natural resources and multiethnic population give the country the potential to become a leading nation in Central Asia and the world.

Above: **Kazakh women sell apples in a park in Almaty. The city is famous for its many apple trees.**

Almaty

The city of Almaty was the capital of Kazakhstan from 1929 until 1997. During the Soviet years, the city was known as Alma-Ata. Almaty is situated at the foothills of the towering Zailiysky Alatau, at an elevation of about 2,135 feet (650 m), in the southeastern corner of Kazakhstan. Most views of the city also contain the spectacular snowcapped summits of the Alatau. Almaty is a garden city, with many parks and wide avenues lined with flowering plants and trees. The Kazakhs named the city after the many apple trees that grow in the area. In fact, *Almaty* literally means "father of apples" in the Kazakh language. Two rivers flow through the city.

History

Almaty has played an important role in the history of Kazakhstan since ancient times. The city has its origins in an ancient settlement that flourished along the Silk Road. In the thirteenth century, Mongol invaders destroyed the settlement. Almaty

Below: **Almaty's Republic Square boasts a large artificial pond.**

Above: **Almaty has many parks that feature fountains.**

remained a small village until the arrival of the Russians in the 1800s. In 1867, the Russians established the administrative center of the Seven Rivers region in the city, which they renamed Verny. In 1921, the Russians named the city Alma Ata, the Russian version of the Kazakh name, Almaty. After the Soviets came to power, Alma Ata became the capital of Kazakhstan in 1929. In the 1930s and 1940s, the city grew quickly after the building of a railway and factories brought Russian immigrants into the city. In 1986, violent riots took place in the city when Soviet president Mikhail Gorbachev replaced the Communist Party leader of Kazakhstan with the Russian Gennady Kolbin, and many Kazakh protesters were killed. In 1989, Gorbachev replaced Kolbin with Nursultan Nazarbayev, an ethnic Kazakh. After Kazakhstan gained independence, the capital was transferred from Almaty to Astana, in northern Kazakhstan, in 1997.

Kazakhstan's Business Center

Since independence, Almaty has become a bustling international city. Foreign business people have come to Almaty, attracted by the prospects of investment in Kazakhstan.

CULTURAL AND SPORTS CENTER

Almaty boasts eight theaters. The best-known theater is the Abay State Academic Opera and Ballet House. Almaty also houses three major museums, the Central State Museum, the A. Kasteyev State Museum of Fine Arts, and the Republican Museum of Folk Musical Instruments. The Medeo Sports Center, surrounded by views of the Zailiysky Alatau, holds international ice skating competitions.

Ancient and Modern Architecture

Although Kazakhstan's beginnings date back thousands of years, the nomadic Kazakhs built few permanent buildings. Nevertheless, fascinating remains of ancient structures can be found throughout Kazakhstan. In recent years, modern architectural works have sprung up in Kazakhstan's major cities, contrasting with the country's landscape.

Ancient Buildings

The legendary Silk Road, the route that connected China to Europe starting in about 300 B.C., crossed southern Kazakhstan. Towns developed near the Silk Road, leaving remains of mosques, fortresses, and burial structures in southern Kazakhstan.

The oldest structures in Kazakhstan are the burial mounds of warriors found on the Saryarka Plains that date back to before 500 B.C. The remains of several towns that existed between the first and fifteenth centuries A.D. have been unearthed in southwestern Kazakhstan. One of these towns, Otrar Tobe, has buildings made of mud bricks. The city of Taraz houses the mausoleums of Aisha-Bibi and Babadzha-Khatun, both of which date back to the twelfth century. According to legend, Aisha-Bibi was a young beauty who died of a snakebite while on her way to meet her lover in Taraz. Babadzha-Khatun was her companion and guarded Aisha-Bibi's grave until her own death.

Modern Architecture

Russian architecture influenced the military forts built during the eighteenth and nineteenth centuries along the borders of Kazakhstan, in present-day Russia. The Russians also built government offices and churches, the most famous of which is the Orthodox Svyato-Voznesensky Cathedral in Almaty. Although buildings were mostly functional during the Soviet era, some outstanding examples of modern architecture, such as the Medeo Sports Center and the Palace of the Republic, were built in Almaty. A complex of government buildings and a grand mosque were built in Astana, the new capital city, in the late 1990s.

Above: **This new building in Astana houses the parliament of Kazakhstan.**

KHOJA AKHMED YASAVI MAUSOLEUM

Khoja Akhmed Yasavi (1103–c.1166) was an Islamic scholar who lived in Turkestan for most of his life. A respected and popular preacher and poet, a small mausoleum was built for him upon his death. His current mausoleum was built near Turkestan in the fourteenth century. The building houses more than thirty-five rooms. Mosaics decorate the walls of the mausoleum.

Opposite: **Designed by Russian architect Andrei Zenkov and built in 1904, the Orthodox Svyato-Voznesensky Cathedral is a striking example of Russian architecture prior to World War I.**

The Aral Sea

The Aral Sea is a large, shallow, saltwater lake located in southwestern Kazakhstan, on the border between Kazakhstan and Uzbekistan. Vast deserts and plains completely surround the lake. In the 1960s, the Aral Sea was the fourth-largest inland lake in the world, with an area of 26,250 square miles (68,000 square km). Due to misuse of the lake's water sources, however, the Aral Sea has now been reduced to a third of its original size, while the amount of water in the lake is now less than a quarter of its former volume.

THE ARAL SEAS?

The drastic reduction in water in the Aral Sea caused the lake to split into two by 1989. In recent years, the lake has split into three parts: the Small, or Northern Sea; the Central Sea; and the Western Sea, most of which is in Uzbekistan.

Above: The dried-up lake bed of the Aral Sea is crusted with salt.

Background

The Aral Sea is located in an area that has cold winters, hot summers, and an annual average rainfall of 4 inches (100 mm). In the 1950s, the Soviet Union embarked on an ambitious plan to cultivate cotton as a cash crop in the region. To irrigate the vast plains for agricultural purposes, many canals were built to draw water from the Amu Darya, which flows from Uzbekistan, and the Syr Darya, the two rivers that feed the Aral Sea. By the 1980s, during the summer months, both rivers were drying up before reaching the sea. As a consequence, the water in the lake is evaporating faster than it can be replenished.

Environmental Damage

Many serious problems have resulted from the reduction of the Aral Sea. As the amount of freshwater flowing into the lake from the two main rivers has decreased, the salt level in the lake has increased. As a consequence, the water in the Aral Sea is no longer fit for drinking or supporting large amounts of fish. The fishing industry in the area, which once harvested large quantities of sturgeon, carp, and other fishes, is almost completely gone.

Water and air pollution are two other serious problems in the Aral Sea region. In addition to salt, the Aral Sea's waters have a high content of pollutants, mostly pesticides used in the nearby

INTERNATIONAL COOPERATION

NATO's Division of Scientific and Environmental Affairs and the German Remote Sensing Data Center have pledged funding to improve land and water use in the area around the Amu Darya.

agricultural fields. As parts of the lake have dried up completely, parts of the Aral Sea's lake bed, which contain high levels of salt and chemicals, have become exposed. As a result, winds blowing over the Aral Sea carry millions of tons of salty dust and chemicals to areas around the lake, causing air and water pollution. Skin and respiratory diseases are also affecting the people living near the lake. Children suffer most from this pollution. In the regions close to the Aral Sea, the infant mortality rate has reached 100 for every 1,000 births. Experts predict that unless strict corrective measures are put in place, the Aral Sea might disappear by the year 2020.

Above: As the waters of the Aral Sea recede, ships anchored in the Aral's seaports have become stranded in the middle of a dried lake bed.

Anatoli Boukreev

Anatoli Boukreev, a Russian-born mountain climber from Kazakhstan, achieved international fame in May 1996 after rescuing some members of an expedition to Mount Everest that claimed the lives of eight climbers.

Early Life and Achievements

Anatoli Boukreev was born on January 16, 1958, in Korkino, a town located in the southeastern foothills of the Ural Mountains, which lie on the vast Russian steppes near the border with Kazakhstan. At age twelve, he started mountaineering and rock-climbing training in the Ural Mountains. In 1974, Boukreev began rigorous training in the Tien Shan, scaling peaks averaging 16,400 feet (5,000 m). Boukreev earned a college degree in physics in 1979. After serving in the Mountaineering Division of the Soviet Army, Boukreev made his home in Almaty, Kazakhstan, where he spent most of his adult life. After the collapse of the Soviet Union, Boukreev became a Kazakhstani citizen.

Below: **Anatoli Boukreev (*left*), a world-class mountaineer, was also an accomplished cross-country skier.**

Boukreev led many expeditions to the Tien Shan in Kazakhstan, the Himalayas in Nepal, and many other ranges. He holds the distinction of having reached the summit of the highest peaks in the world without the aid of supplemental oxygen.

Tragedy in the Himalayas

On May 10, 1996, Boukreev was one of the leaders of an expedition to Mount Everest that was organized by a U.S.-based tour company. Tragically, eight members of the expedition lost their lives. Boukreev single-handedly managed to rescue three of the lost climbers, however. Although he was fiercely criticized by some for his actions during that tragic expedition, Boukreev received the David A. Sowles Memorial Award, the highest award given by the American Alpine Club, in December 1997 for his rescue efforts on Mount Everest.

On Christmas Day 1997, Boukreev died in an avalanche while climbing Annapurna, also in the Himalayas. President Nazarbayev awarded Boukreev a posthumous Order of Personal Courage of the Republic of Kazakhstan.

Above: **Climbers camp out in tents at Mount Khan-Tengri's base camp. Boukreev led many expeditions like this one to the Tien Shan Mountains.**

JOURNALS ON BOUKREEV'S LIFE

During his life, Boukreev contributed articles to different mountaineering magazines and spoke about his experiences as a mountain climber. Two books are available on his life. *The Climb*, coauthored by Boukreev and G. Weston Dewalt, describes the events on the tragic expedition to Everest in 1996. *Above the Clouds* is a collection of his journals, published posthumously in 2002.

The Deserts of Kazakhstan

Deserts occupy a large part of Kazakhstan's vast territory. Deserts and semiarid lands stretch across the country from the Caspian Sea in the west to the foothills of the Dzungarian Alatau in the southeast. The Saryarka Plains extend to the north of this area. Clay, stone, salt, and sand cover these deserts.

The major rivers that flow through the deserts of Kazakhstan are the Chu and the Syr Darya. Two other rivers running through the country's deserts are the Ili and the Karatal, which flow into Lake Balkash in the Seven Rivers region.

Sand Deserts

Sand deserts, such as the Myunkum in southern Kazakhstan; the Kyzylkum, bordering Kazakhstan and Uzbekistan; the Aral Karakum; and the Barsuki in northern Kazakhstan, cover huge areas of the country. The northern parts of the Myunkum, Kyzylkum, and the Barsuki have very cold winters. These deserts are exposed to the icy Arctic winds, which sometimes cause sandstorms. Sand wormwood, an aromatic plant; sand sedge,

Left: **This impressive canyon in southeastern Kazakhstan is known as the Valley of Castles. The canyon's sharp angles and rugged surface resemble castle walls and towers, which have given the canyon its name. The Charyn River runs through deserts, mountains, and these canyons before its waters fall into the Ili River.**

a type of grass; and saxaul, a woody shrub, among other hardy plants, grow in these regions.

Stone and Gypsum Deserts

The vast Ustyurt Plateau, with an area of 77,200 square miles (200,000 square km), lies between the Caspian Sea and the Aral Sea. To the west of Lake Balkash, the Betpak-Dala Desert stretches over an area of 29,000 square miles (75,000 square km). Rubble and pebbles cover the surface of these deserts. Under the surface of the Betpak-Dala, shallow layers of gypsum, a soft mineral used in plaster and as a fertilizer, are found. Underground water sources are also found in these areas, but as the water is far out of the reach of plants, vegetation is sparse. Nevertheless, in the past, Kazakh nomads herded their animals to the Ustyurt Plateau to graze on the plateau's vegetation. The Betpak-Dala was also used as pastureland in spring and fall. The Ustyurt and the western part of the Betpak-Dala do support wormwood and shrubs.

Environmental Problems

Kazakhstan suffers from many environmental problems. These environmental problems have caused serious health and social problems for the people of Kazakhstan. Most of these problems are the direct result of the government's harmful industrial and agricultural practices during the Soviet era.

Air, Water, and Land Pollution

The Soviet-era government's various large-scale agricultural programs caused the reduction of large bodies of water and desertification, as well as air, water, and land pollution. The most severe case of water reduction has taken place in the Aral Sea. The dried-up lake beds of the Aral now hold large amounts of salt and pollutants. When blown by the wind, these pollutants contaminate the air, water, and land in other areas. People breathing the air and drinking the water in these polluted areas

THE CASPIAN SEA

In contrast to the Aral Sea, which has lost much of its water, the Caspian Sea has been experiencing a rise in its water level since 1978. In addition to the Caspian Sea being rich in marine life, the area around the sea is rich in oil. If the Caspian Sea's water level continues to rise, scientists fear that the nearby oil fields will be flooded by the year 2020.

Below: Canals have diverted the flow of rivers in Kazakhstan.

have suffered from a variety of diseases connected to pollution, and the lands have become unfertile as a result of the high levels of salt in the soil.

Industrial pollution is another major problem in Kazakhstan. Soviet-era factories currently functioning in Kazakhstan's larger cities still use old machinery and outdated technology. These factories are responsible for releasing toxic gases into the air and into the ground, affecting underground sources of water. Large cities, such as Almaty, suffer from air pollution caused by exhaust from old vehicles and poor traffic control.

Nuclear Testing

One of the most serious environmental problems in Kazakhstan is nuclear radiation. From 1949 to 1989, the Semey area, formerly known as Semipalatinsk, was used as a testing ground for nuclear weapons. The effects of radiation on the population living in the area have been disastrous. Thousands of people have died from radiation-related illnesses. The number of cases of leukemia and other types of cancer is unusually high. The infant mortality rate and the number of children born with defects is also high.

Above: **These children in Astana play near a polluted stream.**

ENVIRONMENTAL PROGRAMS

In 2001, Kazakhstan's Ministry of Environmental Protection established the Regional Environmental Center (REC) in Almaty. The center's aim is to promote cooperation between the public and the Central Asian republics on issues concerning the environment. The European Union and the United States have provided funds and technical support to help Kazakhstan protect its fragile environment.

Kazakh Games

The nomadic past of the Kazakhs is evident in the traditional games of Kazakhstan. As both Kazakh men and women rode on horseback to herd their livestock across the steppes, many Kazakhs are accomplished riders. Many of Kazakhstan's traditional games involve horseback riding.

Horseback Wrestling

Wrestling on horseback, or *audaryspak* (ow-dahr-is-PAHK), is a tough sport involving hand-to-hand combat between two men riding on horseback. The rider who succeeds in wrestling his opponent until the opponent falls off his horse is the winner.

Kokpar

In the past, Kazakhs believed that they could protect themselves from evil by sacrificing goats. Fighting for the carcass of a goat, known as *kokpar* (kok-PAHR), is an ancient sport. Held on a vast open steppe, goals are lined up at opposite ends of the field. Two teams of horsemen must pick up the goat's carcass and throw it into the opponent's goal. The player who has gotten hold of the goat carries it over his shoulder and gallops at full speed, while the opposing team's players try to snatch the goat away from him. A live goat is sometimes used instead of the carcass of a goat.

Picking Up the Coin

Kumis alu (koo-MISS ah-LOO) literally means "picking up the coin." In this game, a rider has to pick up a handkerchief from the ground while riding at full speed. In the past, the horseman had to pick up a silver coin, explaining the name of the game.

Catch the Girl!

Known as *kyz kuu* (khyz KHOO), in this lively competition, a young man on horseback pursues a young lady riding ahead of him. She has to prevent him from getting ahead of her. As soon as he draws near, she gives him a lash of the whip. He has to persist, but if he is still unable to catch up with her by a fixed point in the race, he gets another lashing. However, if he manages to overtake her, he gets a kiss from the girl as a reward.

Above: **The Kazakhs, who are known as excellent horse riders, have created elaborate saddles from leather and metal.**

Opposite: **Two Kazakh men, dressed as traditional Kazakh warriors, get ready to take part in kokpar.**

Multiethnic Nation

For about two hundred years, Kazakhstani society has consisted of several different ethnic groups, including Russians, Ukrainians, Uzbeks, Germans, and Koreans. This demographic makeup was the direct result of Russian, followed by Soviet, occupation of the country from the early 1800s to the late 1900s. By the second half of the twentieth century, ethnic Kazakhs had become a minority in their own country. Since the early 1990s, thousands of non-Kazakh Kazakhstanis have left the country, while ethnic Kazakhs have returned from abroad and resettled in Kazakhstan.

Problems with Emigration

Since independence, several laws that emphasize the importance of Kazakh culture have been passed in Kazakhstan. For instance, the Kazakh language is now the state language in the country, and knowledge of it is a requirement for university entrance. Due to these new laws, members of minority ethnic groups feel that they are at a disadvantage when compared to the Kazakhs. As a result, between 1989 and 1999, more than 1.5 million Russians and

LANGUAGE ISSUES

Since independence, Kazakhstan has passed a law that requires everyone applying for a job in the government to be fluent in the Kazakh language. Ethnic Russians and other non-Kazakhs feel that this law discriminates against them and favors ethnic Kazakhs.

Below: **Most cities in Kazakhstan have a multiethnic population.**

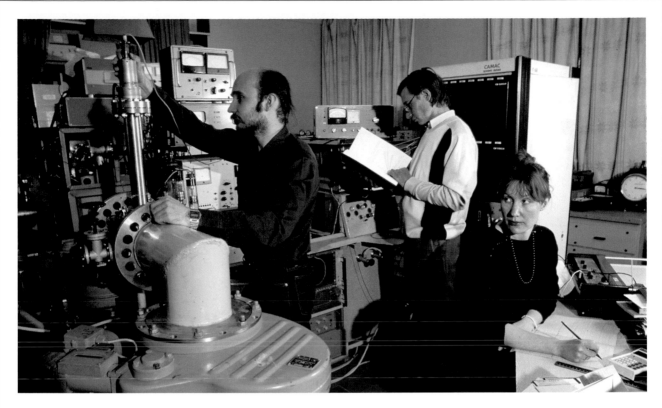

more than 500,000 Germans left Kazakhstan. As German law grants citizenship to ethnic Germans regardless of place of birth, most Kazakhstani Germans have emigrated to Germany. As the cost of resettling these ethnic Germans into German society has been very high, the German government has promised to provide financial support for Kazakhstani Germans, to encourage them to stay in Kazakhstan. More than a third of Kazakhstan's Ukrainian population and great numbers of Kazakhstanis of other ethnic groups have also left the country. As the economic situation in Kazakhstan has improved, however, some Kazakhstani Russians who left for Russia have returned to Kazakhstan.

Returning Kazakhs

As many as 60,000 Kazakhs from Mongolia and many Kazakhs from China have returned to Kazakhstan over the last few years. Many of these repatriates resettled in northern Kazakhstan, where they were employed as herdsmen. As the economic situation in rural Kazakhstan has been difficult since the early 1990s, many rural Kazakhs have not welcomed the repatriates. They feel the repatriates are taking jobs away from them. Communication is also a problem, since most repatriates do not speak Russian.

Above: **Kazakhstanis of Russian and German descent form a large part of the country's skilled workforce.**

ETHNIC TENSION

Although Kazakhs and Russians have, for the most part, lived side by side peacefully in Kazakhstan, many Kazakhs feel that the Russians made the Kazakhs a minority in their own homeland. Millions of Kazakhs either starved to death or left the country as a result of Soviet policies. Nuclear testing has also damaged the lives of thousands of Kazakhs.

Musical Instruments and Oral Epics

Oral epics have served as the basis of Kazakh culture. These epics are an art form that requires great musical talent from the storytellers that perform them, because musical accompaniment forms an important part of the Kazakh epic tradition.

The Oral Epic

In the days before formal education was introduced, Kazakh nomads learned about their history and culture through the legends, epics, songs, and poems performed by a special person known as a zhyrau, or epic singer, who is always a specially trained man. In ancient times, the zhyrau occupied an important place in tribal society as adviser to the khan. The zhyrau

THE DOMBRA

Of all traditional Kazakh instruments, the dombra is the most popular today. The traditional dombra has two strings made of sinew, although a modern dombra may have nylon strings. Kazakh singers play the dombra to accompany epic songs.

Left: An epic singer holds a dombra. When playing the dombra, singers usually either strum or pluck the strings.

commanded great respect in the tribes because of his knowledge of Kazakh history and traditions. The akyn was a poet-improviser who represented a clan or tribe in the aitys competitions. Unlike the zhyrau, the akyn did not deliver lyrical or religious poems and could be a man or a woman.

Kazakh epic songs tell of the exploits of legendary heroes and are narrated in different ways. Some of their lyrics not only tell but also comment on the deeds of the heroes. Other lyrics are meant to inspire the audience to action or reflection. In fact, the main aim of this tradition is to deliver a moral. During the performance, an exchange takes place between the performer and the audience. The listeners are not just spectators. They are expected to participate by responding to the views presented.

Traditional Kazakh Musical Instruments

Over the centuries, the Kazakhs developed many kinds of musical instruments, such as the *shankobyz* (shahn-koh-BEEZ), the *sybyzghy* (soo-biz-GHEE), the *kobyz* (koh-BEEZ), and the dombra. The shankobyz is a women's instrument, similar to a mouth harp. The sybyzghy is a wooden instrument that consists of two flutes bound together with a string. The kobyz is an instrument similar in shape to the dombra. The kobys, however, is played like a cello.

Nauryz

The biggest and most festive holiday in Kazakhstan's calendar, Nauryz takes place every year on March 22. For Kazakhstanis of all ethnic groups, Nauryz symbolizes the arrival of spring after the long, cold months of winter, as well as the beginning of a new year. In fact, Nauryz is also called *ulys kuni* (oo-LEES koo-NEE), which means "the first day of the new year" in Kazakh.

Origins of Nauryz

Nauryz is a holiday that probably originated in Persia long before the arrival of Islam. Nauryz marks the vernal equinox, or the new year according to the solar calendar. The first mention of Nauryz in Kazakhstan dates back to the 1700s. Although the Soviets at first banned all religious practices, the government revived the celebration of Nauryz in Central Asia in the last decades of the Soviet era. Because Nauryz was associated mostly with nature and activities such as farming and livestock breeding, the Soviets used Nauryz as a holiday to unite all the ethnic groups in Kazakhstan, regardless of religion. In present-day Kazakhstan, Kazakhstanis of all ethnic groups celebrate Nauryz.

NAURYZ BELIEFS

Most traditions related to Nauryz are based on the belief that the way one celebrates Nauryz will influence the year ahead. Traditional Kazakhs make peace with their enemies, clean up their homes, and prepare lavish meals for their guests on Nauryz. Kazakhs believe that the more generously they behave during Nauryz, the richer they will be in the coming year.

Seven is a very important number during Nauryz. Dishes include seven ingredients, which are water, salt, wheat, millet, meat, sour cream, and dates. Respected elders of the community, called *ak sakal* (AHK sah-KAHL), meaning "white beards," are given a place of honor in the public celebrations. Seven bowls of *nauryz khoze* (now-REEZ k-HOH-ZAY), a soup made from seven types of grains, are placed in front of them. White is also a very symbolic color in Nauryz. The elders often wear white turbans, and many of the yurta on display are white.

Left: A young girl, dressed in bright traditional Kazakh attire, performs a song during Nauryz celebrations in Almaty.

Celebrations in Kazakhstan's Big Cities

In cities, Nauryz celebrations have a modern and multiethnic flavor. In Almaty, performers stage concerts, traditional Kazakh dances, and singing contests in the city's public squares and theaters. Games and rides for children are set up in public parks, along with stalls selling snacks and sweets. Horse races are held in Almaty and other big cities. Yurtas are set up in parks so people can experience traditional Kazakh dwellings. Bands play many kinds of music, from traditional Kazakh tunes to pop songs from the United States.

Celebrations in Rural Kazakhstan

In the rural areas of southern Kazakhstan, where the population is mostly Kazakh, Nauryz celebrations are focused on Kazakh and Islamic traditions. Men and women dress up in richly brocaded outfits, while children wear velvet vests. The celebration begins with a prayer, in honor of ancestors, recited in the town square by an Islamic religious teacher. After the prayer, traditional Kazakh games on horseback and aitys competitions begin.

Above: **During a Nauryz celebration, people sit down around a *dastarkhan* (dass-tark-HAHN), a table or cloth, laid out with several meat dishes, noodles, bread, and sweets. Food plays a major part in Nauryz celebrations, and women prepare elaborate dishes for their families and guests.**

63

Nursultan Nazarbayev

Nursultan Abishevich Nazarbayev, Kazakhstan's president, was born in 1940. He was born to a family of peasants in a rural village in the Almaty province. He graduated from a technical school in metallurgy and worked as a steelworker and engineer. In 1962, Nazarbayev joined the Communist Party of the Soviet Union (CPSU), and by 1969, he had become an official of the CPSU in Kazakhstan. After holding various prominent posts in the CPSU, he became chairman of the Kazakh Council of Ministers in 1984.

In 1986, Soviet leader Mikhail Gorbachev decided to remove longtime Kazakh leader Dinmukhamed Kunayev from the position of first secretary of the Kazakh Communist Party, the top political position in Kazakhstan. Citing corruption as the reason for this decision, Gorbachev replaced Kunayev with Russian leader Gennady Kolbin. Kazakhs violently opposed this decision and started riots in Almaty. In 1989, Gorbachev transferred Kolbin to Moscow and appointed Nazarbayev to the top position in Kazakhstan.

Left: **President Nursultan Nazarbayev waves to a crowd of supporters in Almaty on Republic Day, October 25, 2002.**

The Soviet government assigned Nazarbayev to the new position of president of the Kazakh republic in 1990. In December 1991, after the collapse of the Soviet Union, Nazarbayev became the first president of the independent country of Kazakhstan.

Above: **Russian leader Vladimir Putin (*left*), Chinese leader Jiang Zemin (*center*), and Nazarbayev (*right*) met in Almaty in 2002 at the first Conference on Interaction and Confidence Building Measures in Asia (CICA) summit.**

Nazarbayev's Policies

After the Kazakh culture was suppressed under the Soviets, President Nazarbayev, an ethnic Kazakh, is eager to see the culture once again become mainstream in Kazakhstan. He is also aware, however, of the fact that the Russians form a large part of the country's population and contribute significantly to the economy. Thus, Nazarbayev has been trying to make the Russians and other groups feel that they still have a place in Kazakhstan; the Russian language, for instance, continues to be an official language. Nazarbayev has also been careful to keep good relations with Russia, as the two countries share strong historical and linguistic ties. At the same time, Nazarbayev has also forged ties with other countries, such as Turkey, the other Central Asian states, Germany, the United States, Japan, and South Korea.

Traditional Clothing

Traditional Kazakh clothing is made of colorful materials and is decorated with elaborate embroidery that resembles the design on the national flag. Although most Kazakhs wear traditional clothing only on festive occasions, such as weddings or Nauryz, some people in rural areas still don traditional clothes daily. Traditional Kazakh clothes, which suit the country's harsh climate, have changed little over the centuries. These clothes are often made from fabrics woven from camel and sheep's wool.

Traditional Clothes for Women

Traditional clothing worn by Kazakh women uses many different materials and designs. Red is a popular color among Kazakh women. A Kazakh woman's outfit consists of a long, straight dress and a pair of loose pants. The outfit is completed by a sleeveless vest called a *beshmet* (besh-MEHT), which is made of heavy cotton, wool, silk, or velvet. To keep warm, Kazakh women wear a cotton undershirt. In winter, women wear jackets and coats made of wool or fur.

KAZAKH WEDDING DRESSES

A Kazakh bride wears a long, white silk gown embroidered with gold or silver threads. A red beshmet is worn over the dress. The bride wears a *saukele* (sou-keh-LAY), a tall, cone-shaped hat made of thin felt and richly decorated with feathers, gold threads, beads, and sometimes, jewels. A long veil, which is meant to cover the bride completely, hangs from the top of the saukele. The embroidery on the dress, beshmet, and saukele always match.

Left: Kazakh vests worn by women are richly embroidered with felt patterns and colorful designs.

Kazakh women wear a wide variety of hats and other headgear. What a woman wears depends on her age and status in society. Some women wear caps decorated with a fur band around the brim. The saukele, a cone-shaped felt hat lined with expensive fabric and decorated with beads, precious stones, and other ornaments, is worn by young women on very special occasions. Girls can decorate their saukele as they please, and some girls add feathers to the top. Traditionally, married women covered their head, most often with a scarf, when going outdoors. Rural Kazakh women still follow this tradition regularly.

Above: **These rural Kazakhs are wearing traditional long woolen robes, leather boots, and fur caps with earflaps.**

Traditional Clothes for Men

For work, men wear a cotton shirt and long pants tucked into high leather boots. Over this outfit, men also wear a knee-length, fitted, quilted robe that can be sleeveless or long-sleeved. In winter, men wear long, embroidered coats made from sheepskin. To withstand the harsh winters on Kazakhstan's steppes, men wear fur caps. These caps have earflaps and are made from lamb's wool. On festive occasions, Kazakh men sometimes wear a pointed, black-and-white felt hat.

Traditional Economy

Before the twentieth century, many Kazakhs led a nomadic lifestyle. The Kazakh nomads lived by raising livestock, which they herded to pastures across the vast steppes of Kazakhstan. To Kazakh nomads, their livestock was their most valuable possession. Kazakhs derived their food, clothes, shelter, and other items of daily use from their livestock.

Livestock Herding

Before the arrival of the Russians, Kazakh nomads followed a fixed herding route that had been marked out for the different tribes by the khan. These routes varied depending on the season and available pastures. Kazakh nomads traveled with their entire family by horse or camel. Their possessions, including their yurtas, were often carried in a cart pulled by donkeys or yaks.

In the mountainous regions, Kazakh nomads spent winters in the valleys of the mountain rivers. In summer, they moved higher, into the cooler mountain meadows.

Below: **Although most Kazakhs no longer lead a nomadic lifestyle, some present-day Kazakhs do sometimes camp out in a yurta for a few months, in order to look for grazing land for their animals. These "nomads," however, also have permanent homes in towns or villages.**

As soon as they arrived at a destination, Kazakh nomads set up camp, putting up their yurta near a river or any other source of fresh water. Traditionally, the men looked after the livestock and were also in charge of milking the mares, while women did all the domestic chores.

Above: **In the rural regions of Kazakhstan, farmers raise cattle for their milk and meat. In the past, cattle was most often raised by Kazakhs who did not lead a nomadic lifestyle, as cattle cannot travel long distances.**

Handicrafts

During the winter months, Kazakh nomads spent more time in their yurtas, as grazing pastures dry out in winter. Men and women spent this time making all their necessary household items. Both men and women took part in tanning leather and skins from their animals and made clothing, shoes, and saddles. Women were in charge of processing sheep's wool, while woodwork and metalwork were done exclusively by men. The Kazakhs used wood to build yurta frames and trunks, all of which were required for their nomadic lifestyle. Metal was used for making weapons, household utensils, and tools and instruments. During Soviet times, these crafts almost died out, but they have been revived since independence.

Women in Kazakhstan

Women have always played important roles in Kazakh society. Traditionally, Kazakh women had to work very hard. Nomadic women took care of the yurta and children, in addition to helping out with the animals. Women also made carpets and clothing. Certain practices in traditional Kazakh society, such as bride kidnapping, have made Kazakh women's position in society vulnerable. Unlike in more strict Muslim societies, however, the nomadic Kazakh lifestyle gave women the freedom to take part in horse races and singing contests. In Kazakh epic tales, women characters are just as clever and courageous as male characters.

During Soviet times, traditional practices such as polygamy and bride kidnapping were illegal. Girls received the same education as boys, and women became active in the workforce. During that time, both Kazakh and Russian women played an active role in the economy. Since independence, the government's tendency to reject the Soviet system in favor of Kazakh traditions may have a negative effect on women, as old customs such as bride kidnapping have made a comeback in the last decade.

Left: **An elderly nurse provides assistance to a young mother and child in a clinic near the Aral Sea. The environmental problems caused by the reduction of the Aral Sea have affected the health of women and children in particular.**

Challenges for Kazakhstani Women

Since independence, women in Kazakhstan have faced many challenges. As a result of the economic downturn experienced by the country during the first years of its independence, thousands of women lost their jobs. As many child care centers have also closed down, mothers cannot look for work outside the home, reducing family incomes even further. When families in Kazakhstan experience financial difficulties, the tendency in the family is to give priority to the educational needs of sons rather than daughters. As a consequence, women's opportunities for economic improvement decrease even further.

Single mothers in Kazakhstan are also in a very difficult position, with limited welfare services and child care centers. The situation for rural women is more critical than for city women as fewer jobs are available in the countryside.

Women's representation in Kazakhstan's government remains low. In 1998, women held a little more than 11 percent of the seats in the Majilis. In 2004, this percentage had increased only slightly.

Above: These Russian Kazakhstani women have set up a small shop in Astana. They make and sell ornaments made from dried flowers.

Yurtas

Since ancient times, yurtas have been the traditional dwellings of the Kazakhs. These collapsible tents perfectly suited the nomadic lifestyle as they are easy to assemble and transport. Although yurtas are rarely used as a year-round dwelling today, they continue to be a symbol of Kazakh culture. A circular structure with a dome-shaped roof, yurtas are able to withstand strong winds as well as the weight of the snow that accumulates during the long winters in Kazakhstan.

Structure of a Yurta

A yurta has a dome-shaped roof supported by a framework of curved, collapsible panels of latticed wood. These panels are covered with felt for warmth and protection. Long, curved poles are attached to the upper part of the panels. The upper ends of these poles are gathered into a wooden hoop, which gives the yurta its dome shape. A felt flap on top of the hoop is tied back

Below: **A yurta is warm in winter and cool in summer. Flaps around the bottom border of the yurta can be lifted open to allow cool breezes to come in during the hot summer months.**

to form an opening for smoke from the cooking stove. The stove is usually placed slightly off-center, closer to the door.

Above: **The floor of a yurta is usually covered with felt carpets, and its walls are decorated with colorful rugs.**

Types of Yurtas

There are different types of yurtas for different types of people. In the past, wealthy people's yurtas were usually white, which symbolized prosperity and good health. Common people's yurtas were black. A newlywed couple lived in a smaller yurta. Today, a shepherd's yurta is very simple and much smaller than most others. It consists of straight poles stuck in the ground and bound together at the top, giving it a conical shape.

Arrangement of Furniture

Everything in a yurta had a functional and decorative purpose. The interior of a rich family's yurta was a breathtaking display of beautifully carved and inlaid chests, handmade carpets, and embroidered furnishings. Women usually sat near the entrance, while the men sat along the walls farthest from the entrance. A stove was placed near the center, and the space near it was usually reserved for a guest of honor.

RELATIONS WITH NORTH AMERICA

During the Soviet years, Kazakhstan had no direct diplomatic relations with either the United States or Canada. After the collapse of the USSR, Kazakhstan's president, Nursultan Nazarbayev, opened up the country to foreign investment and diplomatic relations. Kazakhstan's enormous size, strategic location in Central Asia, and rich natural resources make the country an influential nation in the region. The United States and Canada realize the importance of having strong relations with Kazakhstan in order to make possible safe investment and defense partnerships in Central Asia.

Opposite: **A poster for the U.S. blockbuster film *Titanic* stands on a street in Almaty. U.S. films are very popular in Kazakhstan.**

Some international human rights groups, however, have fiercely criticized Kazakhstan's harsh treatment of political opponents and President Nazarbayev's methods of staying in office. These groups have asked the leaders of the United States and Canada, in writing, to put pressure on President Nazarbayev to improve Kazakhstan's human rights record. Neither the United States nor Canada has issued open criticism of President Nazarbayev's policies. Instead, both Canada and the United States continue to pursue close economic and cultural ties with Kazakhstan.

Above: **President Nazarbayev (*seated, left*) and U.S. president George H. W. Bush (*seated, right*) signed an economic and security agreement during Nazarbayev's visit to the White House in May 1992.**

Strengthening Relations

Relations between Kazakhstan and the United States have been strong and stable ever since the two countries established diplomatic ties in 1991. Shortly after Kazakhstan declared independence from the Soviet Union in December 1991, the United States was the first nation in the world to recognize it as a sovereign state. In January 1992, the United States opened an embassy in Almaty. In May of the same year, Kazakhstan opened an embassy in Washington, D.C.

Both countries reap benefits from this relationship. Kazakhstan's rich and, as yet, undeveloped oil and other energy resources make the country an attractive place for U.S. investment. Kazakhstan, on the other hand, benefits from U.S. assistance and expertise in developing democratic institutions, a free-market economy, and policies on environmental protection.

President Nazarbayev has paid several official visits to the U.S. president in Washington, D.C. The first two visits, in 1992 and 1994, were mainly concerned with the elimination of Kazakhstan's nuclear weapons arsenal. High-ranking U.S. government officials have also visited Kazakhstan in recent years.

Below: President Nazarbayev (*far left*) and President George W. Bush (*right*) met in the United States in December 2001. At the end of the visit, Kazakhstan and the United States pledged to strengthen cooperation between the two countries to fight terrorism, promote peace, prevent the spreading of nuclear weapons, and build a free-market economy in Kazakhstan based on democratic rule.

Left: U.S. secretary of state Colin Powell (*right*) shakes hands with Kazakhstan's foreign minister, Erlan Idrissov (*left*), during the latter's visit to Washington, D.C., in December 2001.

Financial and Technical Assistance

Since 1992, the United States has offered Kazakhstan a wide range of economic, technical, cultural, and humanitarian assistance. The United States, through the U.S. Agency for International Development (USAID), is helping the government of Kazakhstan develop a sound financial policy, as well as commercial laws, that will enable the country to make a smooth transition into the global market. The United States has also provided assistance to help improve Kazakhstan's health and educational services, as well as to help fight pollution and dispose of radioactive substances used in making nuclear weapons. In addition, Kazakhstan's military has taken part in joint training with the U.S. armed forces.

Kazakhstan has also received aid, in the form of loans, from the World Bank. These loans were aimed at helping with the process of privatizing formerly state-owned businesses. The World Bank continues to provide loans to Kazakhstan to help the country improve its infrastructure and environment. In 2002, the World Bank opened its Central Asia Regional Office in Almaty.

Nuclear Weapons

The most important factor that has ensured smooth relations between Kazakhstan and the United States has been Kazakhstan's willingness to dispose of its arsenal of nuclear weapons and weapons of mass destruction, which had been developed by the Soviet government.

On May 23, 1992, Kazakhstan and the United States signed the Strategic Arms Reduction Treaty (START) in Lisbon. By signing this treaty, Kazakhstan showed serious commitment to eliminating its nuclear weapons and becoming a nonnuclear nation. This commitment was further strengthened by the signing of the nuclear Non-Proliferation Treaty, in 1993, and the Comprehensive Test Ban Treaty, in 2001.

With help from the United States, Kazakhstan has succeeded in eliminating all of its weapons of mass destruction. All nuclear weapons have been dismantled. Kazakhstan also closed down all nuclear weapons factories and transferred tons of uranium, a substance used in making nuclear weapons, to the United States for safe storage.

Below: This rocket, which was launched in July 2000 from the Baikonyr space center in western Kazakhstan, was part of a space mission. Since Kazakhstan's agreement to destroy all of its nuclear weapons, some rockets built to deliver nuclear missiles have been used for peaceful purposes.

Left: **President Nazarbayev (*right*) welcomes U.S. secretary of state Madeleine Albright (*left*) during the latter's visit to Astana in April 2000.**

Security and Defense

The United States has been eager to develop military ties with Central Asian nations since the mid-1990s. In 1995, with support from the United States, Kazakhstan and its neighbors, Kyrgyzstan and Uzbekistan, formed the Central Asian Battalion (Centrazbat), a military unit that takes part in peacekeeping operations in Central Asia. The United States military has held training exercises in Kazakhstan and Uzbekistan for Centrazbat.

Military and defense cooperation between Kazakhstan and the United States was formalized when the two countries signed a defense cooperation plan during a ceremony at the Pentagon in Washington, D.C., on December 17, 1999. According to this plan, the United States pledged to provide military training and expertise to Kazakhstan's armed forces; the United States also agreed to help Kazakhstan keep security at its borders.

In light of the terrorist attacks of September 11, 2001, and the recent wars in Afghanistan and Iraq, the United States has reinforced its interest in Central Asia, partly because of the region's proximity to the Middle East. In 2002, after a visit by U.S. secretary of defense Donald Rumsfeld during the war in Afghanistan, Kazakhstan agreed to let the U.S. air force use Almaty's airports for emergency landings.

U.S. Companies in Kazakhstan

During the long period of Soviet communist rule, all of Kazakhstan's means of production — agricultural land, farms, and factories — belonged to the state. After the Soviet Union collapsed and Kazakhstan became independent, all industries in Kazakhstan lost Soviet support. In order to save the country's industries and create jobs for the population, Kazakhstan opened the country to foreign investment and privatized a number of major companies.

U.S. businesses were among the first to begin investing in Kazakhstan's industries. Philip Morris, a major U.S. tobacco company, acquired the Almaty Tobacco Company in 1993. Philip Morris now controls 80 percent of Kazakhstan's tobacco market.

Two other U.S. multinational companies have a major presence in Kazakhstan. Procter & Gamble, the huge manufacturer of family and household care products, opened an office in Kazakhstan in 1994. Coca-Cola began distributing soft drinks in Kazakhstan in 1996.

Above: The use of modern agricultural equipment made by U.S. companies, such as John Deere and Case IH, has helped to improve Kazakhstan's agricultural output.

Kazakhstan's agricultural output declined greatly after independence, as a result of outdated machinery and inefficient technology. The agricultural industry, however, has great potential in a large country such as Kazakhstan, and two major U.S. makers of agricultural machinery, John Deere and Case IH, have been introducing modern machinery into Kazakhstan since the late 1990s.

Tengiz Oil Field

Kazakhstan's biggest draw for foreign investors is the country's rich natural resources. Kazakhstan has enormous reserves of oil, gas, and other fossil fuels, but the country needs foreign investment in order to develop these resources. U.S. multinational oil companies, such as Chevron and ExxonMobil, have invested in the development of the Tengiz oil field — one of the largest oil fields in the world — located off the northeastern shore of the Caspian Sea. Chevron, along with other European and U.S. firms, has also invested in the Caspian Pipeline Consortium (CPC). In March 2001, the CPC completed a pipeline to transport crude oil from the Tengiz oil field to a Russian port on the Black Sea.

INVESTMENT CHALLENGES
Kazakhstan's vast economic potential has attracted billions of dollars in foreign investment to the country. Foreign firms, however, have faced challenges when working in Kazakhstan. The country's infrastructure remains largely undeveloped, so multinational companies have been asked to put extra money into projects such as building schools and hospitals. Some observers also worry about government corruption.

Left: The Caspian Sea holds vast oil reserves. Oil companies extract oil from the lake using offshore oil rigs. This photo shows part of an oil rig as it is being towed to its final position in the lake.

U.S. Aid in Fighting Pollution

The United States has provided Kazakhstan with assistance to deal with the country's environmental problems. The Central Asia branch of the USAID has provided technical assistance to help improve water management in the Syr Darya river basin. In 2001, the United States, in cooperation with the European Union (EU) and the Ministry of Environmental Protection in Kazakhstan, helped establish and fund the Regional Environmental Center (REC), an independent nonprofit organization, in Almaty. The REC aims to educate the people in Kazakhstan and Central Asia about the importance of preserving the environment and ways to put environmental policies into practice. The United States has also agreed to cooperate with Kazakhstan in tackling the damage done to the Aral Sea and Semey's nuclear testing grounds. The United States has begun work to clean up an island on the Aral Sea that was used by the Soviets to test biological weapons. To dispose of the uranium that was left after the removal of all nuclear weapons from Kazakhstan, the United States transported some uranium to the United States for reprocessing.

Below: **An abandoned ship sits on the Aral Sea's polluted, dried-up lake bed.**

Democratic Institutions

Although the constitution of Kazakhstan is based on democratic principles, many international observers believe that the government of Kazakhstan has not put these principles into practice. For instance, the president has the power to start constitutional reforms, which should then be approved by the Constitutional Council. Because the chairman of the council is also appointed by the president, observers believe that constitutional changes can be passed easily without the vote or participation of democratically elected representatives. Kazakhstan's human rights record has also been severely criticized. Journalists and editors who have been critical of the government have reportedly been harassed by what some people believe are government forces.

Some observers feel that the United States, as a strategic economic partner, should put pressure on President Nazarbayev to build up democratic institutions. They argue that the U.S. government has avoided issuing public accusations of President Nazarbayev and making specific demands of the government of Kazakhstan because of the economic ties between the two countries and Kazakhstan's support of the war on terrorism.

Above: **A Peace Corps volunteer conducts a small-business training program among farmers in rural Kazakhstan.**

U.S. PEACE CORPS IN KAZAKHSTAN

The first team of U.S. Peace Corps volunteers arrived in Kazakhstan in 1993. Apart from teaching English, the volunteers work on environmental projects. Peace Corps workers also offer advice on managing and developing small businesses in a free-market economy. As of late 2003, there were more than 120 Peace Corps workers in Kazakhstan.

The Central Asian–American Enterprise Fund

In order to encourage the development of the private sector in Central Asia, U.S. president Bill Clinton set up the Central Asian–American Enterprise Fund (CAAEF) in 1994. The CAAEF provides loans to Central Asian companies, especially small- and medium-sized businesses in countries that show commitment to implementing free-market reforms. The CAAEF also offers technical support to these businesses.

Educational Links

Educational ties between the United States and Kazakhstan have developed over the last decade. In 1997, the Kazakh–American University was established in Kazakhstan as the first independent university in the republic. The university, which is modeled on American universities, offers classes in English and gives Kazakhstani students the chance to study in universities in the United States. In 1993, the University of Kentucky founded the Kazakh–American Studies Center. The aim of the center is to establish close ties with government agencies and institutes of higher learning in Kazakhstan.

SOROS FOUNDATION

Founded by Hungarian-born American financier George Soros (*left*), the Soros Foundations offer scholarships for study in U.S. universities to Kazakhstani students and teachers.

Left: **President Nazarbayev (*right*) is welcomed by Canadian prime minister Jean Chretien (*left*) during Nazarbayev's visit to Canada in June 2003. Chretien, who stepped down as prime minister in December 2003, has been serving as a special advisor to Petro-Kazakhstan, a Canadian oil company doing business in Kazakhstan.**

Relations with Canada

Canada has strong commercial ties with Kazakhstan. Canada conducts more trade with Kazakhstan than with any other Central Asian nation. In 1996, Canada opened an embassy in Kazakhstan. Although Kazakhstan has no embassy in Canada yet, Kazakhstan's embassy in Washington, D.C., also serves Canada. Members of Canada's parliament visited Astana and Almaty in May 2000; in 2002, the Canadian secretary of state for Central and Eastern Europe and the Middle East paid a visit to Kazakhstan during a tour of Central Asia.

In 1996, Canada and Kazakhstan signed a trade agreement, which included agreements on taxation for both countries. Canadian firms that have invested in Kazakhstan have mostly been oil and gas companies. Petro-Canada was involved in the exploration and discovery of an oil field in Kazakhstan in 1995. The oil field began production in 2002.

Environmental Projects

The Canadian government, through the Canadian International Development Agency (CIDA), supports projects that focus on sustainable development. CIDA has funded training programs on the development of water resources in the Aral Sea basin. CIDA has also sponsored agricultural training programs for Kazakhstani farmers and forest conservation programs.

KAZAKHSTAN

International Boundary
Province Boundary
■ **Capital**
● **Major Town**
～ **River**
▲ **Mountain**

RUSSIA

Petropavlovsk

SOLTUSTIK (NORTH)
KAZAKHSTAN

Kostanay

Kokshetau

Lake
Seletytengiz

Irtysh ● Pavloda

Uralsk (Oral)

Tobyl

KOSTANAY

Turgay
Plateau

Ishim

AKMOLA

■ ASTANA

● Ekibastuz
Ekibastuz Basin

PAVLODAR

Chingiz

BATYS (WEST)
KAZAKHSTAN

Ural

Aktyubinsk ●

AKTOBE

Arkalyk

Lake Tengiz

● Karaganda

Kazakh Uplar

ATYRAU

Caspian Depression

● Emba

Mugodzhari Hills

Ulutau Mountains

Saryarka
Plains

KARAGANDA

Atyrau ●

Emba

Barsuki Desert

Aral ●

Aral Karakum
Desert

Betpak Dala Desert

Balkash ●

Lake Balkast

Balka
Bas

Tengiz
Oil Field

KYZYLORDA

● Baikonyr

Chu

ZHAMBYL

Ili

Tengiz ●

Caspian Sea

MANGGHYSTAU

Ustyurt
Plateau

Tupkaraghan Peninsula

Aral
Sea

Syr Darya

● Kyzylorda

Myunkum
Desert

Tien Sh

● Shu

Aktau ●

Karagiye Basin

Kyzylkum
Desert

ONGTUSTIK (SOUTH)
KAZAKHSTAN

● Taraz

Amu Darya

Otrar Tobe ●

● Turkestan

KYRGYZSTAN

Shymkent ●

UZBEKISTAN

TURKMENISTAN

TAJIKISTAN

E

N

Semey

SHYGHYS (EAST) KAZAKHSTAN

Oskemen

Altai Mountains

Lake Zaysan

Zaysan

Lake Alakol

Lepsi

ALMATY

Baskan

Aksu

Dzungarian Alatau

arakand

atal

Charyn

Bi

Seven Rivers

Valley of Castles

ountain Range

Almaty

Chimbulak

iliysky Alatau

Mount Khan-Tengri
(22,949ft / 6,995m)

CHINA

Akmola C1–D2
Aksu River E3
Aktau A3
Aktobe A2–C3
Aktyubinsk B2
Almaty (city) E3
Almaty (province)
    D2–E3
Altai Mountains E2
Amu Darya B3–C4
Aral B3
Aral Karakum Desert C3
Aral Sea B3
Arkalyk C2
Astana D2
Atyrau (city) A3
Atyrau (province) A2–B3

Baikonyr C3
Balkash D3
Balkash Basin D3
Barsuki Desert B3
Baskan River E3
Batys (West) Kazakhstan
    A2–B2
Betpak Dala Desert
    C3–D3
Bi River E3

Caspian Depression
    A2–A3
Caspian Sea A3–A4
Charyn River E3
Chimbulak E3
China E2–E4
Chingiz-tau Range
    D2–E2
Chu River C3–D3

Dzungarian Alatau E3

Ekibastuz D2
Ekibastuz Basin D2
Emba (city) B2
Emba River A3–B2

Ili River D3–E3
Irtysh River D1–E2
Ishim River C1–D2

Karaganda (city) D2

Karaganda (province)
    C2–D3
Karagiye Basin A3–A4
Karatal River D3–E3
Kazakh Upland D2
Kokshetau C1
Kostanay (city) C1
Kostanay (province)
    B1–C2
Kyrgyzstan D3–E4
Kyzylkum Desert C3–C4
Kyzylorda (city) C3
Kyzylorda (province)
    B3–C4

Lake Alakol E2
Lake Balkash D3–E2
Lake Seletytengiz D1
Lake Tengiz C2
Lake Zaysan E2
Lepsi River E3

Mangghystau A3–B4
Mount Khan-Tengri E3
Mugodzhari Hills B2–B3
Myunkum Desert D3

Ongtustik (South)
    Kazakhstan C3–D4
Oral A2
Oskemen E2
Otrar Tobe C4

Pavlodar (city) D1
Pavlodar (province)
    D1–E2
Petropavlovsk C1

Russia A4–E1

Sarakand River E3
Saryarka Plains C3
Semey E2
Seven Rivers region E3
Shu D3
Shyghys (East)
    Kazakhstan D2–E3
Shymkent D4
Soltustik (North)
    Kazakhstan C2–D1
Syr Darya B3–D4

Tajikistan C4–D4
Taraz D3
Tengiz A3
Tengiz Oil Field A3
Tien Shan mountain
    range D3–E3
Tobyl River B2–C1
Tupkaraghan Peninsula
    A3–A4
Turgay Plateau B2–C2
Turkestan C4
Turkmenistan A4–C4

Ulutau Mountains
    C2–C3
Ural River A2–A3
Uralsk A2
Ustyurt Plateau A3–B3
Uzbekistan B3–D4

Valley of Castles E3

Zailiysky Alatau E3
Zaysan E2
Zhambyl D3–D4

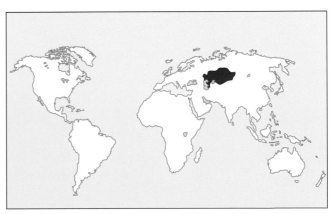

KAZAKHSTAN

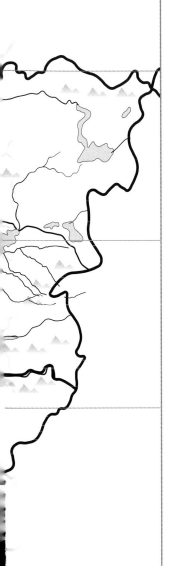

How Is Your Geography?

Learning to identify the main geographical areas and points of a country can be challenging. Although it may seem difficult at first to memorize the locations and spellings of major cities or the names of mountain ranges, rivers, deserts, lakes, and other prominent physical features, the end result of this effort can be very rewarding. Places you previously did not know existed will suddenly come to life when referred to in world news, whether in newspapers, television reports, other books and reference sources, or on the Internet. This knowledge will make you feel a bit closer to the rest of the world, with its fascinating variety of cultures and physical geography.

This map can be duplicated for use in a classroom. (PLEASE DO NOT WRITE IN THIS BOOK!) Students can then fill in any requested information on their individual map copies. The student can also make a copy of the map and use it as a study tool to practice identifying place names and geographical features on his or her own.

Above: **A yurta's walls consist of latticed wooden poles.**

Kazakhstan at a Glance

Official Name   Republic of Kazakhstan

Capital   Astana (since 1997)

Official languages   Kazakh (state) and Russian

Population   16.8 million (July 2003)

Land Area   1,030,810 square miles (2,669,800 square km)

Provinces   Almaty, Akmola, Aktobe, Atyrau, Batys (West) Kazakhstan, Mangghystau, Ongtustik (South) Kazakhstan, Pavlodar, Karaganda, Kostanay, Kyzylorda, Shyghys (East) Kazakhstan, Soltustik (North) Kazakhstan, Zhambyl; and three cities of equal status to provinces, Almaty, Astana, and Baikonyr

Major Cities   Almaty, Astana, Karaganda, Pavlodar, Shymkent

Highest Point   Mount Khan-Tengri 22,949 feet (6,995 m)

Major Lakes   Aral Sea, Caspian Sea, Lake Balkash, Lake Tengiz, Lake Zaysan

Major Rivers   Chu, Ili, Irtysh, Syr Darya, Tobyl, Ural

Ethnic Groups   Kazakh (53.4 percent), Russian (30 percent), Ukrainian (3.7 percent), Uzbek (2.5 percent), German (2.4 percent), Uighur (1.4 percent), other (6.6 percent)

Main Religions   Muslim (47 percent), Russian Orthodox (44 percent)

Public Holidays   New Year's Day (January 1), International Women's Day (March 8), Nauryz (March 22), Day of Unity of Peoples of Kazakhstan (May 1), Victory Day (May 9), Constitution Day (August 30), Republic Day (October 25), Independence Day (December 16)

Major Exports   Chemicals, grain, machinery, meat, metals, oil, oil products, wool

Major Imports   Foodstuffs, machinery, metal products

Trade Partners   China, France, Germany, Italy, Russia, Ukraine, United States

Currency   Tenge (143.6 KZT= U.S. $1.00, February 2004 estimate)

Opposite: **The Independence Monument adorns the Republic Square in Almaty.**

Glossary

Kazakh Vocabulary

aitys (eye-TEES): a contest in which two singers improvise witty lyrics back and forth in response to each other's lines.

ak sakal (AHK sah-KAHL): "white beards"; elders in the community.

akyn (ah-KIN): a Kazakh singer and poet-improviser. Plural: akyndar.

alyp qashu (ah-LIP kah-SHOE): "bride kidnapping"; a traditional Kazakh practice in which a man kidnaps a woman and marries her.

audaryspak (ow-dahr-is-PAHK): a Kazakh game in which two men on horseback wrestle until one falls off his horse.

batyr (bah-TEER): a Kazakh warrior who fought against the Mongol invaders.

berkutchi (behr-koot-SHE): a sport that involves training a golden eagle to hunt.

beshbarmak (BESH-bahr-mahk): "five fingers"; the national dish of the Kazakhs, which consists of boiled meats served over noodles.

beshmet (besh-MEHT): a traditional Kazakh vest worn by women that is usually made of velvet or silk and embroidered with intricate designs.

boza (boh-ZAH): a Kazakh alcoholic drink made from millet.

dastarkhan (dass-tark-HAHN): a table or cloth laid out with meat dishes, bread, and sweets.

dombra (dome-BRAH): a Kazakh musical instrument similar to the lute.

kalym (kah-LEEM): "bride price"; the money paid by the parents of the groom to the bride's parents, usually in an arranged marriage.

kazakh (kah-ZAHK): "free and independent nomad."

kazy (KAH-zee): smoked horseflesh sausage, a Kazakh specialty.

kokpar (kok-PAHR): a Kazakh sport, in which two teams of numerous riders compete to control the carcass of a goat and throw it past a goal post.

kumis alu (koo-MISS ah-LOO): "picking up the coin"; a Kazakh game in which a player tries to pick up a handkerchief from the ground while riding on horseback. In the past, a silver coin was used instead of a handkerchief.

kobyz (koh-BEEZ): a Kazakh two-stringed wooden musical instrument.

kymyz (kur-MWEEZ): a fermented beverage made from mare's milk.

kyz kuu (khyz KHOO): "catch the girl"; a Kazakh game in which a girl and a boy, each on horseback, try to outrun each other. If the girl wins, she gets to whip the boy; if the boy wins, he gets a kiss from the girl.

Majilis (mah-jee-LEES): Kazakhstan's lower house of parliament.

Nauryz (now-REEZ): a spring festival celebrated in Central Asia and some countries in the Middle East.

nauryz khoze (now-REEZ k-HOH-ZAY): a Kazakh soup made from seven types of grain, often served during Nauryz.

oblystar (oh-blees-TAHR): provinces. Singular: oblys.

Oraza Ait (OH-rah-zah AH-eet): a feast that celebrates the end of Ramadan, the Islamic month of fasting.

saukele (sou-keh-LAY): a cone-shaped Kazakh hat worn by girls that is made of felt and decorated with elaborate embroidery, jewels, and feathers.

shankobyz (shahn-koh-BEEZ): a Kazakh musical instrument similar to a mouth harp.

sybyzghy (soo-biz-GHEE): a Kazakh wooden flute.

ulys kuni (oo-LEES koo-NEE): "the first day of the new year"; another name for the Nauryz festival.

Zhetysu (JAY-tee-soo): "seven waters"; the Kazakh name for the Seven Rivers region.

zhus (ZHOOZ): literally "one hundred"; a large nomadic tribe.

zhyrau (jeer-OW): a Kazakh epic poet.

Russian Vocabulary

borsch (BOHRSH): a hearty soup made from meat boiled with beets, cabbage, potatoes, and sour cream.

manti (mahn-TEE): a large dough pocket filled with meat, onions, and, occasionally, pumpkin.

orda (ohr-DAH): a large group of unrelated nomadic family clans under the leadership of a khan.

pelmeni (PEL-me-nee): a Russian dish that consists of meat and onion dumplings.

pilaf (PEE-laf): a rice dish made with carrots, mutton, and oil; or with dried fruit, raisins, and prunes.

plov (PLOFF): another name for pilaf.

Semirechie (SEH-mee-REH-chee-eh): "seven rivers"; the Russian name for the Seven Rivers region.

Arabic Vocabulary

Eid Al-Adha (EED ahl-ahd-HAH): the Muslim "feast of the sacrifice," in which a sheep is slaughtered and its meat shared with the poor in the community.

Eid Al-Fitr (EED ahl-feetr): the festival that celebrates the end of Ramadan, the Islamic month of fasting.

English Vocabulary

a cappella: singing without musical accompaniment.

bravura: daring performances.

cash crop: an agricultural product for which there is great market demand.

demographics: statistical data on a country's population that is organized by ethnic and social divisions.

desertification: the process by which an area of land becomes a desert.

indigenous: originating in or characteristic of a specific location.

khanates: Central Asian nations ruled by the descendants of Genghis Khan.

mausoleum: a large building where one or several tombs are placed.

nomadic: having no permanent home and moving from place to place.

purges: removals from a government or a political organization.

repatriates: people who have returned to their homeland after living abroad.

secular state: a country governed by civil authority rather than religious authority.

sedentary: living in one place for a long period of time.

steppe: a vast plain without trees.

More Books to Read

The Atlas of Islam: People, Daily Life and Traditions. Neil Morris (Barrons Educational Series)

Attila and the Nomad Hordes: Warfare on the Eurasian Steppes 4th–12th Centuries. Elite series, No. 30. David Nicolle (Osprey Publishing Co.)

The Fall of the Soviet Union. Miles Harvey (Children's Press)

Genghis Khan. Ancient World Leaders series. Brenda Lange (Chelsea House)

Kazakhstan. Cultures of the World series. Guek-Cheng Pang (Benchmark Books)

Kazakhstan. Modern World Nations series. Zoran Pavlovic (Chelsea House)

The Mongol Empire. World History series. Mary Hull (Lucent Books)

Monuments of Central Asia: A Guide to the Archaeology, Art and Architecture of Turkestan. Edgar Knobloch (I. B. Tauris)

Spreading Deserts. Green Alert series. Paul A. Rozario (Raintree)

Threatened Habitats. Green Alert series. Uma Sachidhanandam (Raintree)

Videos

Central Asia. Globe Trekker series (555 Productions)

Kazakhstan: Jouldouz in Kazakhstan. Let's Dance series (Marathon International)

Russia, the Caucasus & Central Asia. Standard Deviants School: World Geography series (Cerebellum Corp.)

Web Sites

www.encyclopedia.com/html/a/arals1ea.asp

www.kazakhembus.com

www.kazakhstan-gateway.kz/?lang=en

www.odci.gov/cia/publications/factbook/geos/kz.html

www.president.kz/

Due to the dynamic nature of the Internet, some web sites stay current longer than others. To find additional web sites, use a reliable search engine with one or more of the following keywords to help you locate information about Kazakhstan. Keywords: *Aral Sea, Astana, Central Asia, Genghis Khan, Kazakhs, Nursultan Nazarbayev, Scythians, Tien Shan.*

Index